GENTLEMEN
PREFER ASIANS

D1600547

GENTLEMEN PREFER ASIANS

*Tales of Gay Indonesians
and Green Card Marriages*

Yuska Lutfi Tuanakotta

ThreeL Media | Berkeley, California

Published by
ThreeL Media | Stone Bridge Press
P. O. Box 8208, Berkeley, CA 94707
www.threelmedia.com

© 2016 Yuska Lutfi Tuanakotta.

Edited by Jill Kolongowski.

Book design and layout by Linda Ronan.

All rights reserved.

No part of this book may be reproduced in any form without permission from the publisher.

Printed in the United States of America.

p-ISBN: 978-0-9964852-0-3
e-ISBN: 978-0-9964852-2-7

My endless gratitude to those who have made this book a reality. Terima kasih.

Contents

LOT'S WIFE

We hoard memories like a rodent preparing for winter. We hoard them in objects like a movie or a song or a color or a sunset or a white pair of Fruit of the Loom boxers or words like "toxic" and "passive-aggressive" and "codependent." Sometimes an object holds so many memories that they overflow, and if one were to sort through them one might find dried pieces of cat poop wedged between the box of little kisses and the box of angry shouts.

Our memories don't care what we're doing. A split second of idleness and they occupy. They take over when we're sitting on the toilet, or when we're lying down waiting for sleep, or when we're doing our night run. Even when we're supposed to be focusing on an activity, like driving or having sex. They invade, they push around, jab their elbows at the present, like teenagers in their mosh pits, seeking anarchic attention. Me, me, me. Look at me, listen to me, but don't fucking touch me. Oh look, I made you run through a stop sign. Bad driver. Must be Asian.

Our memories attack us. They come out of nowhere, they blindside. I was slicing a satsuma open, and its scent filled my nostrils. The next thing I knew I was crying over a night long gone, in a country where I was born, when it was humid and searing hot, and my mother—that small Asian woman—had placed satsumas in the fridge, knowing full well that they would cool the throats of her family so we could go through the night without turning on the air conditioner and racking up the electricity bill.

Our memories metastasize. They attach and associate. They network like hungry politicians. Some associations are simple and self-explanatory: airports mean pilots, Indonesia means family. Some are cryptic and personal: full moon means a dead cat, *Practical Magic* means a best friend, UC Berkeley means assholes. Some are just as bizarre and as pareidolic as finding Jesus' face on a piece of toast. I was at Singapore's Changi Airport walking to my boarding gate to fly home to Jakarta when I realized that I might be walking the same path, stepping on the same carpet, perhaps even sitting in the same chair as The Baker whenever he flew back to Jakarta on his yearly Southeast Asian backpacking trip. It didn't matter that Changi had three terminals and hundreds of boarding gates.

Our memories are shape-shifters. They change their stances like opportunistic friends. They are bipolar. They go from positive to negative to good to bad to cherished to a weapon until we can't decide what they really are anymore and we don't know how to categorize them, which explains why I now hate Christmas.

Our memories are like fig trees. Their roots dig deeply into the past and their branches and leaves reach up to the future. They leap across minutes, months, and years, from the first flirt to the last straw.

Our memories are jet-setters, astronauts, farers of universes. Our memories don't care for boundaries or visas or green cards or immigration rules or TSAs. They slap us from behind pictures on postcards and places on television screens. Every trip to a Chinese market is like flipping through a family album. Every Facebook post, every Tweet, every goddamn article on the Internet needs to have a trigger warning.

And eventually, little by little, those memory boxes will disappear. Forcefully cleaned out. Thrown away. Eventually, we'll find ourselves unable to recognize people anymore, unable to verbalize what we want to say, unable to do simple tasks, unable to find the bathroom in our own house, and we'll end up crapping ourselves. But there will still be boxes we hold on to until our last breath—the boxes that house precious fragments from our lives.

THE ENABLER

One of my earliest fragments was of my father and me.

It was a strange day. Strange because I was spending it alone with my father. I can't remember where my mother was. I was five or six and I'd spent most of my time with her. My father was about forty-three and I remember his hair was still thick and jet black.

We were at a department store in Jakarta, riding up the single-file escalator to the upper level—the kids' section.

As I got off the escalator, I saw an island of piles and piles of Goggle-V costumes, folded and wrapped in plastic. Goggle-V is a band of masked Super Sentai heroes, a predecessor of Power Rangers. I was in love with Goggle Pink. And by in love, I mean I worshipped her and wanted to be her.

I scanned the island for Goggle Pink's costume and finally found it. It was just a flimsy, shapeless, spandex jumpsuit with Velcro on the back, no shoes nor mask. But it was just as magical. I asked my father if I could try it on. He called a salesperson to find one in my size.

Other fathers buy their five-year-old sons robot toys or miniature cars or fake guns or rubber bows and arrows. That day, I came home wearing a pink spandex superhero jumpsuit and a pair of pink-rimmed plastic sunglasses that my father thought went with the costume.

ARIO

Los Angeles was hotter than the Human Torch's asshole that Sunday. I'd driven over to Glendale in The Musician's car to see Ario. It was to be our second meeting. The first one had been a week before, when Ario's husband, The Sculptor, hired me to photograph his latest pieces. He told me he was married to an Indonesian, and I, always needy for a real-life conversation in my native language, had tried to talk to Ario. But he had been elusive, only peeking once into The Sculptor's workroom. Then he sent me an email, saying he'd gotten the address from his husband, and he knew I'd wanted to talk to him. He told me we could talk if I could bring Djarum, Indonesian clove cigarettes. "I haven't smoked it in years," he wrote.

The yard of their Glendale house had patches of unkempt weeds and dandelions that created a lush, green illusion. The door swung open before I knocked.

"Do you have it?" Ario said. He had a British accent. He wore a teal tank top. His long, wiry arms hung loose. Golden-copper colored. I nodded and handed him the pack that I'd stolen from The Musician's stash. He'd bought a carton of them on his trip to Indonesia. Ario grabbed the pack and walked away from the door. I trailed behind. "*Tutup pintunya*," he said, and I closed the door behind me.

"All they have here are shitty American cigarettes,"

Ario said. "Fuck this country and its whole anti-cigarette sentiment." I followed him to the patio in the backyard. It was just as unkempt as the front. He lit one and took one long, Zen inhale, and blew it out. "So good."

I coughed. "Sorry," I said.

"Don't apologize. I should be the one apologizing for killing you with this."

"You're alone?"

"Yeah. The whore's out."

"The who?"

"The whore," Ario said. "My husband."

Ah.

Ario took another nicotine swig.

"So," he said.

"So," I said.

"I saw your portfolio," he said. "Not bad. I bet you had fun taking nude photos of those guys."

"Oh, well, I'm not Terry Richardson."

"Good."

"You know who he is?"

"Sure. I follow fashion. And good job on my husband's sculptures too."

I nodded.

"You know he fucks his models, don't you?"

"Terry Richardson?"

"No," Ario rolled his eyes. "I couldn't care less what he does. I was talking about my husband."

I looked away. I remembered The Sculptor saying a thing or two about his pieces, twelve to thirteen inches of white gypsum sculptures with wire skeletons. "This one was of this boy," The Sculptor had said and showed me a nude photo of the model taken in his sculptor room. An Asian, twenty-something. "Nice ass. Nice dick, too. Oozing precum like a leaking faucet," The Sculptor said.

I'd looked away then and faux-fumbled with my camera, the way one would do with a phone or paper napkins when nervous.

"Every. Single. One of them," Ario said.

The scarce September breeze helped move the hellish Los Angeles air along.

"Did he fuck you?"

"Excuse me?" I said. "No. I mean, I was there to take photos. And besides, come on. Really? Look at you. I can't compete with you. Not with your cheekbones and your smooth skin and your great teeth and that body." Sweat made the tank top cling to Ario's skin, and it showed that he worked out.

Ario smiled and nodded, not an insincere or a cynical smile, but a sheepish realization that he was overestimating me. I half-expected him to say something along the lines of, "Aw, you shouldn't have. You're also very attractive." But he didn't. And I felt resentment for about five seconds.

We talked about Berkeley. Ario used to live no more than five blocks away from my apartment. He had a master's degree in French.

"It's peculiar, isn't it?" Ario said. "Going to America to learn French?"

"I came here to study belly dancing, but don't tell my mother," I said.

"I don't know your mother." Obviously the joke fell flat.

"It's more peculiar that we never crossed paths."

Ario inhaled his cigarette while he looked at me like an *okiya* owner inspecting a girl who wanted to become a geisha.

"You're writing a book," he said. "About your life.

About your marriage to this American, about abandoning your family, your friends, your country, in search of love, of a better life. Or shortcut to a better life." Ario squished his cigarette into the ground and lit another one. "Why?"

"I don't know," I said.

"But you do," he said. "What is it? Fame? Money? A chance to shit-talk your exes? All of the above?" Ario cocked his head and smiled at me. Then he turned away to blow the smoke.

"I'm worried that it will ruin my relationships," I said. "I'm also worried about what people will think of the book."

"That's if people actually think of the book."

Yes. Thank you. "I'm worried it may end up like *Fifty Shades of Grey*. Or *Twilight*. Or *The Hunger Games*. Or *The Bell Jar*. Or that novel about Mata Hari. Or any of Nicholas Sparks' books. Or worse: *Eat, Pray, Love*."

"Which Mata Hari novel?"

"It's sad. I found a copy at a bookstore in Berkeley. Mint condition, labeled as used. Obviously the previous owner hadn't bothered to read it. I picked it up because of the title: *The Red Dancer*."

"Because you belly dance."

I nodded.

"And?"

"I only read the first ten pages," I said. "It was horrible. A fictional recounting of Mata Hari from people close to her. I mean, she is a nice subject and all, but she's been beaten to death."

"More like shot to death, am I right?" Ario said. I laughed out of politeness. "But yeah. She's just like mummies in movies. They've been done so many times before. I had the misfortune of sitting through *Tale of the Mummy* recently."

"I don't know that movie."

"Oh, the usual curse thing. But instead of it being the mummy that goes around killing people, it's the wrapper."

"The wrapper?"

"The mummy wrapper," Ario said. "The fabric. The linen. You know, the cloth. Apparently the fabric absorbs the evil of the mummy and starts murdering random people."

"A killer maxi pad? That's new," I said. I was glad when Ario laughed. You'd think that with all the heat and the cigarette, the ice would've melted a long time ago.

"Terrible acting, terrible script, terrible CGI. Even that gorgeous Chinese guy, Jason Scott Lee, with his naked, oily, awkwardly writhing, delicious body didn't help."

"Full frontal?" I said.

"Back."

"Pity."

"Oh, it has Shelley Duvall in it too." Ario said. "At a séance."

Of course.

"Anyway, how is *Eat, Pray, Love* worse than the others?"

"Because it's critically acclaimed," I said. "And yet it's garbage. I mean, at least E. L. James doesn't go about being smug about a work that's so full of shit."

Ario clicked his tongue. "Wow, so much hate. Why is there so much hate for *Eat, Pray, Love*? I mean, I get that it's about a privileged, dumb, white American who exoticizes the East, and Europe, but what's your excuse?"

"I wasted thirty minutes of my life trying to read it."

"And you've never read *Fifty*?"

I shook my head.

"Well there you go," Ario said. "Maybe this book will end up like *Fifty Shades of Grey*: critically loathed, thrashed by people who haven't read it, yet it spawned two more novels and all three have topped bestseller lists around the world. Or maybe this book will end up like *Eat, Pray, Love*: critically acclaimed, a commercial success, changed many people's lives, and still being hated on. Or maybe this book will end up like that Mata Hari book, a lonely book that nobody reads, and those who do read it will think the author has written, without success, about subjects that have been discussed so many times before. Proof that you can't please everyone. And *The Bell Jar*? Nothing more than pure juvenile indulgence now, is it? It's only famous after she offed herself. Same with van Gogh and his splotchy paintings. Same with Kurt Cobain and his generic music."

Years ago, I probably would have wanted to defend *The Bell Jar*. I probably would've wanted to grab Ario's tank top and scream that unlike Kurt Cobain, Sylvia Plath was a genius, a mad genius, an angry genius. After all, she and the book were my very reasons for wanting to get an MFA in creative writing. But Ario was right—after my third time reading the book, I realized it was terrible. Her poems and the stories in *Johnny Panic and the Bible of Dreams*, on the other hand, are fantastic. And I still regard Plath's *Unabridged Journal* as my holy scripture.

"Are you going to kill yourself after the release of your book?" Ario said.

I shook my head no.

"What if no one buys it?"

No.

"What if it gets negative reviews?"

Still no.

"What if it ruins relationships?"

"I don't know," I said. I don't know. "I'll think about it."

"You want my story," he said, "so you don't have to write about yours. So you don't have to worry about yours."

Long tobacco ash hung from the tip of the burned Djarum cigarette. Ario flicked it away and cursed. "What a waste." He took one last swig and put it out the same way he'd put out the other one.

"I'll give it to you," he said. "I've nothing to lose."

PERSEPHONE

The grand church was dark. In fact, it was dark all around Jakarta. The flash flood from two days earlier had besieged the city. It had destroyed the dam near Ario's house and the church, and flooded the electricity feeder switch that powered his area. For two days, they were left with no electricity, no water, and worst of all, no Internet.

On one of those dark days, Ario's sister got married. She was about to turn forty-two. It was her first marriage, and her husband's second after his first wife's death. The husband was a primary school teacher in a remote village in West Java. The ceremony at the church was candlelit and quiet. They sang hymns unaccompanied by the grand pipe organ. The air conditioner and the ceiling fans were dead. Heat and humidity procreated under Ario's blazer.

It was a small wedding. Only a dozen of their family members were there, scattered inside the spacious church. He was the witness from their side of the family. He and his mother cried incessantly. He and his sister had been close once upon a time, but they'd gone their separate ways in the last eighteen years. Strangers under one roof. They were twelve years apart.

Ario was sitting next to his sister when he started crying, and he held her hand until she told him he was hurting her.

Her husband took her to his house, in that small, remote village, where he would rape her, threaten to kill her, and tell her, as he was fucking her, that he thought of fucking her mother. This was the last straw that was used as the weapon that finally granted her the divorce after fifteen months of marriage, seven of which were used to hide and plan and fight in court.

A year after the wedding, Ario phoned home from his Berkeley apartment. As he smoked by the front door, he told his mother that he was going to marry an American.

"Are you sure?" she said.

"Yes," he said.

"Where did you meet him?"

"On the Internet. But I've met him in real life since then. A lot of times. And he's kind. He's a copywriter, but he sculpts for a hobby. His workroom is magical. And he cooks too. He made Indonesian fried rice the other day. I still can't believe I actually liked it."

"I just don't want you to make the same mistake your sister did."

But, Ario thought, I wouldn't, would I, Mom? I'm more experienced in this sort of thing. I'm more assertive. I've been dating since I was sixteen.

"He's a good guy." Ario squished the cigarette under his shoe.

MANDALA

"Here," Ario said, "for you."

"What's this?" The Sculptor asked.

Carrying the tube all the way from Berkeley to Oakland was a pain, especially since Ario had to take BART. Then he got into an argument with the people who ran the shuttle service from Oakland to LA because they told him to just "fold the thing." They called him fussy. But he wasn't fussy. He was in love and he didn't think it through.

It was already an inconvenience to paint a project that huge in his shoebox apartment. It only dawned on him when he was two-thirds of the way done that he still had to take it to The Sculptor. But he made the shuttle people make room for the tube. And now there he was, rolling out a seven-by-nine-foot canvas of an oil painting.

It was a smear of red, green, and blue, bleeding into one another. The four gates and the circles were painted with crushed gold leaf that was sealed with clear glue.

"Do you like it?" Ario asked. "It's a mandala."

"I know what it is. Wow. How long did it take you to make this?"

"Ten days," he lied. It took him a month. And that was the third attempt. Those days, it was difficult to walk around his apartment, and the place smelled like oil and turpentine. He had to mask it with Febreze because he was worried his landlord would think of it as a fire hazard.

"I had a bad day today," The Sculptor said. "My friend told me that he saw my ex."

"Oh man. I hate it when people do that."

"Right? But this makes it all better. Thank you."

The Sculptor put on a record. Edith Piaf. "*Hymne à L'amour.*" They danced. Ario remembered crying a little bit. Ario remembered picturing a future, pregnant with possibilities. He would take care of The Sculptor's garden. Find a job. Be domestic. Maybe learn to cook. Maybe get a dog. Or two. A golden retriever and a corgi. Those cute short legs. But not a chihuahua and definitely not a pit bull. They'll have their own little universe. Yes, he'd like that. He'd like all of that.

"Marry me?" The Sculptor asked. They were still dancing, but in silence.

Ario nodded. Perhaps too enthusiastically.

"Yes, I'd like that," he said. I'd like all of that.

MARRIAGE PROPOSAL

If I had truly loved The Baker, we would've been married when he asked me. It didn't matter that Indonesia would not recognize our union. All that would matter was us together. "A small party perhaps," The Baker said, "with just our friends and family."

I balked at the thought of us walking down the aisle, of an unofficial officiant proclaiming us husband and husband.

The Baker asked me to marry him on the sixty-seventh anniversary of the Indonesian Independence Day. The day before The Baker's thirty-second birthday. Three years into our relationship. The president at that time, the worst president the country had ever had, was delivering the Independence Day speech on television. The television was on mute. We were sitting on the edge of the bed in a hotel in Bogor, a little town forty minutes by car from Jakarta. I was there for summer break, and he took days off work and flew from Bali to spend time with me. It was our holiday ritual.

A minute had passed and I still couldn't answer. If that wasn't enough of a sign, I didn't know what was.

I asked The Baker why he wanted to get married.

"To take it to the next step," The Baker said.

"What next step?"

"To be more committed. More serious."

"But we are already committed," I said. "We are already serious."

Three years before, when we became boyfriends, we opened a joint bank account and I had dinner with The Baker's parents. What could be more serious than that?

"Well then," The Baker said, "being married won't be a problem. Right?"

Checkmate. Damn.

"Why can't we stay the way we are?" I said. "We're happy like this."

"I don't understand why you don't want to marry me."

"No, not just you," I said. "If anyone asked me, I would say no. What good will it be in this country?"

The truth was I was afraid of what my mother would say. My parents knew I was gay from the day I was born and they accepted me, but what would she feel if I were married to a man?

The Baker stood up. The mattress shook in anger.

The truth was I didn't love The Baker. Well, I loved him, but not as much as he loved me. Maybe a third of how much he loved me. Maybe even less.

"You're going too fast again," I said. "Remember what I told you about climbing the mountain ahead of me? You've gone too fast, too far ahead, and I'm still down there."

And things like this marriage proposal made me want to leave the mountain more and more.

"All right," The Baker said. "What about an engagement?"

"What do you mean?" I asked.

"Will you be my fiancé?"

That's just as silly, I thought, but I couldn't possibly say that. An engagement sounds less committal. An engagement can be broken off more easily than a marriage. An engagement is half a step forward, not one full one. But maybe it's the only way to save this relationship. If I want to save it. Do I want to save it?

"All right," I finally said. "All right."

The Baker sat down on the bed again and gestured for me to sit on his lap. I obliged and sat facing him. The Baker kissed me.

"We should get a ring," The Baker said.

"No," I said. This time I didn't wait. A nip in the bud.

"Why not?"

"Too frivolous. Let's use the money on something else. Like a vacation."

The truth was I couldn't bear to see those jewelry sales-people looking at us. I thought they would laugh behind my back. "What a silly idea," I imagined them saying. "What a weird-looking couple, but we'll take their money anyway."

But I sensed that The Baker was angry again and I didn't want to anger him. I was glad that I would soon fly back to the US, leaving him again. I would be able to tell The Baker that I couldn't reply to his messages because I was too busy with schoolwork, like I'd been doing when I needed to shut him out for a while.

"We'll see," I said. "If we can find a pair that's not too expensive."

"I love you," The Baker said and kissed me again.

His mouth was too wet, his stubbles were too sharp, his love was too deep.

"I love you," I said, but I knew I didn't mean it, not really.

Within the hour, The Baker changed his Facebook status from "in a relationship" to "engaged" and linked my profile to be approved. I didn't have a choice but to approve it. After my status changed, my Facebook wall was littered with people writing congratulatory notes. I said thank you with many exclamation points, so they would think I was really happy and excited by what was coming ahead. I quietly modified the Facebook setting of my engagement status so that it could only be seen by me and no one else.

A few months after I returned to the US, I began dating other men. One of them was The Pilot.

BUT DO YOU TRUST HIM

I trusted you, was what Adam said to Eve. The gates of Eden had slammed shut behind them.

Why did you say that? Eve thought. I'm not the one who didn't want to give us knowledge. I'm not the one who tried to keep us naked and stupid.

Just like you, Eve said, I was naked and stupid when I gave you that fruit.

Gone was the life of luxury, of leisure frolics. Gone were the days of peace and trotting on cool grass and drinking from the fountain of milk and honey. Now there were sharp gravels and a scorching sun and harsh wind that cut their skin.

They could no longer trust each other. They were alone. Strangers.

Somewhere, Lilith was laughing.

Before track records, before credentials, before credit scores, all we had was our trust instinct. This instinct enabled humans to work together and bring down a mammoth, to welcome a wanderer into their clan, to confide in someone, to say that a piece of plastic was worth a specified amount of paper that was worth a specified amount of gold. Now we need at least three active social media accounts, a year of experience, and three references to even be considered for an entry-level job.

Instincts are like a muscle. They become weak if we don't use them. After thousands of years of civilization, we've been accustomed to science, objectivity, comfort, and tangible evidence before we decide to trust or distrust something. Gut reaction is no longer taken into consideration. Trust instinct can be persuaded by numbers and statistics until we no longer feel the need for it. And so, through evolution, it gradually disappears.

✦✦✦

It was Halloween. The man and the woman were two of the two-hundred-something on board the plane leaving Los Angeles and flying to Cairo.

The seatbelt sign had been turned off. The man kissed the woman's forehead. They were coasting high into clear sky. Turbulence free.

I can't wait, the woman said.

Pyramids, Sphinx, and sand, oh my, the man said.

In seconds, the plane dove nose first toward the waters below. Trinkets and notebooks and pens and glasses floated around them in zero gravity. Electricity and lights went out in the cabin, and the pilot fought to stay alive while the co-pilot fought to die.

The man held the woman's hand. Everything will be all right, he said.

✦✦✦

But it won't be like flying, you say. It's just marriage.

Yeah, but . . .

He's emotionally available, got a good job, steady income,

you say. He has his own house, his own car. It's not flying. It's probably more like driving.

Right. Do you know how many people are killed or become disabled because of drunk drivers, stupid pedestrians, potholes, broken traffic lights? There are literally a million reasons to be afraid of driving.

Okay, well, a walk in the park then, you say.

You might step in dog doo-doo or get bitten by a dog or step on a dog, or get mugged, or killed, or raped.

Then go to a dog-free park.

There's still a possibility of being mugged, or killed, or raped.

Go when the sun's out, you say.

And get skin cancer?

Where's your sense of adventure?

I'll be away. Far away from my family, from my country, from my safety net. Even away from my dance friends and my classmates. I won't know anyone there. How's that not adventure? If anything, it's probably too much of an adventure.

You'll have each other, you say. Isn't that the most important thing?

I guess.

You trust him?

Yes. But the problem is I don't trust myself.

Still, do you realize how easy it is for us to give our trust when we choose to do so?

We trust that the drivers around us aren't drunk or busy texting, that the job advert isn't a spam, that we can pray without someone busting in and shooting at us. We trust that our coworker will return the limited edition director's cut of *The Adventures of Priscilla, Queen of the Desert* Blu-ray disc that she borrowed, that the congressman will do what he promised, that our lover will come get us after having beer with his friends. We trust that the bank won't lose our money, that the house won't lose its value, that our husband won't lose his shit and hit us. We trust that the bridge won't collapse when we're on it, that our childhood TV idol isn't a serial rapist, that it's safe enough to not use condoms. We trust that there's toilet paper after we do number two, that cops won't gun us down senselessly, and that Porgy will find Bess and win her back.

Maybe it's optimism, maybe it's delusion, maybe it's desperation, maybe it's ignorance. Either way, so many things can go wrong.

And what about us? We trust that we're immune to pesticides but not vaccines, that we're cut out to be a mom but not a wife, that we'd rather swim with sharks than deal with a break up, that we're brave enough to dance in front of a hundred people but not to speak in front of one. We trust that we're codependent and toxic and overbearing and aren't worthy to be in a relationship.

The difference between a grown person and a baby is that a baby doesn't have a choice but to trust others to take care of it.

DON'T ASK, DON'T TELL

When my family visited me in Los Angeles in May of 2015, seven months after The Musician and I were married, I asked my mother if she'd told anyone about my marriage.

"No," she said.

"Why not?" I said.

She flicked her wrist once. "Not sure they're ready for that yet."

"No one asks where I am?" I knew I wasn't very popular with my aunts, uncles, and cousins from both sides of the family, what with my odd sense of humor and fashion and reclusiveness, but I couldn't believe nobody had asked.

"Oh, they do," my mother said.

"Then what do you tell them?"

"That you're here, living and working in the US. That's not a lie, is it?"

I shook my head no.

"You've gotten fat," she said. "Look at your belly."

RATE YOUR ACTIVISM

1. You openly defend and fight for queer rights.

2. You defend and fight for queer rights on your own terms (because of lack of time and resources, sometimes not openly, by donating money or services or time to causes, mostly HIV-related). Armchair activists fall in this category.

3. You acknowledge queer people but don't really do anything about it for whatever reasons (don't care, don't have time, don't know anyone who's gay, don't know how to).

4. You privately stand against the movement.

5. You publicly stand against the movement.

NO FEMMES, NO FATTIES,

NO ASIANS

My mother isn't exactly a queer-rights activist. I know she loves me and let me date men and marry one, but she doesn't know the landscape of queer movement in Indonesia, and neither do I. (I know. I'm a disgrace to queer activists everywhere. Although one year, I volunteered to design and maintain the website of Q! Film Festival, Indonesia's annual queer film festival. I also participated in their fringe event by showcasing three illustrations called *The Anatomy of Sissies*, about feminine gay men.) However, my mother's "don't ask, don't tell" approach represents the general idea of LGBT visibility in my country. And that's what I tell foreigners who ask me about the queer-rights movement in Indonesia. We're in the "don't ask, don't tell" era, worried that just discussing it may cause an uproar, and nobody knows for how long. Those who are openly gay are in the very minority, and most of them are like me—we don't have a choice. We're very visible. We stand out like someone who wears neon pink to a white party.

Part of why my activism is limited is because I've always been more interested in genderfuck, in pushing boundaries by wearing makeup and nail polish in public while dressing like a man. My limp wrists are as much a statement as my black Doc Martens boots. I find this to be my own grassroots form of shoving homosexuality, albeit the stereotypically feminine one, in the general public's face.

When I moved to the US, I became more estranged from the Indonesian movement. I tried to reconnect with it when I visited Indonesia in 2013 to do my thesis research on drag queens, but I still felt like an alien.

Another reason for my lack of activism is because I never felt discriminated against. Since I was a child, I've always been ridiculed for being feminine, but not for being gay. In first grade, even before I knew that boys were supposed to be manly, I'd put colored Play-Doh on my nails and pretend I just had a manicure. During my college hazing ritual, my seniors told me to yell, "I can be gay but I can't be feminine!" I learned how Peter must have felt when he denied Jesus. The Monday after hell week ended, I came to campus wearing a bright, canary-yellow shirt at least two sizes too small that I borrowed from a girlfriend.

But it was nothing compared to the ridicule I received from my fellow homosexuals. I was simply too feminine for them. When I was eighteen, my close friend told me, "You know, if only you were manly, you'd have sex more often." Needless to say, he and I grew apart. Fast forward to an era of Internet and touchscreen phones and Grindr is littered with men who specify that they don't want to meet "femmes, fatties, and Asians." I used to only be two of those things, but, since apparently my very own mother thinks I'm fat, I believe I have now hit the jackpot. Ding ding ding indeed.

I'm the stereotype that gay men want to shove back inside the closet. The hysterical, the loudmouthed, the bitchy. The one with the "gay voice." We're feminine and therefore we're embarrassing and not to be taken seriously. But I realize I'm part of a collective, and the needs of this somewhat misogynistic collective triumph over mine.

THE DEMONS OF INDONESIA #1:

BALI

In July of 2015, an American man and an Indonesian man performed a *melukat*, a Balinese Hindu karma cleansing ceremony for couples, at the Four Seasons Resort in Bali. They'd asked the hotel if they could perform a wedding there, but the hotel had refused.

Four months later, the sales executive who brokered the deal was charged by the police for religious blasphemy.

This happened in Bali. The island where Australian tourists go naked and roam the streets in a drunken stupor. The island where there is a street with a row of gay clubs where one could literally club hop. The island where there are clothing-optional hotels.

I wonder what that sales executive was thinking when she authorized the sales. I wonder what she was thinking as she was named a suspect. The couple flew back to the US after the wedding, but not without leaving a trail of a mess.

SAFE

The dressing room of one of Jakarta's two surviving gay clubs was a sea of glitter and dresses and shoes and wigs and feathers and I'd witnessed several gentlemen—bald, scruffy, slender, overweight, short, and tall—paint and contour themselves into Jennifer Lopez, Nicki Minaj, Shakira, Aretha Franklin, and a cast of supporting dancers. I tried to push myself as flat as possible against the wall so I didn't become an intrusion. I was there to observe drag performers, to write their stories for my thesis about the Indonesian drag culture. It was my first stop. Drag queens in their natural habitat: the gay club. That night's theme was Carnival.

"Ten minutes," the club manager called. I gathered my things and came out of the stuffy dressing room.

The gay club itself had changed. I'd arrived several hours before it opened to interview and see these drag performers rehearse. The place was fully lit with unflattering white fluorescent bulbs. I took note of the club's parquet floor, bare ceiling with exposed pipes and air-conditioning units, and the small stage with glitter-dot fabric background. Thanks to lighting, the artificially grungy warehouse had morphed into a darkened upscale club that somewhat justified its ridiculously expensive entrance fee. ("That's how we filter our guests," the club manager said.) It's a tried and true technique with lights (to bring up the good parts) and shadows (to hide the ugly spots). Even the cheap-looking stage was pretty. I sat at the long rectangular bar and watched as people trickled in.

It had been more than a decade since I last went to gay clubs in Jakarta. All of them had gone out of business. I'd been to most of them. They were like mini West Hollywoods. They were full of pretentious people who didn't really dance. They didn't want to get sweaty. They just sat and swayed in their seats, Stepford Boys on steroids, with their designer shirts that hugged their gym bodies and expensive looking drinks in their hands. I went to clubs to dance. When they turned on the lights and started playing last call songs, I'd be drenched in sweat and people would think I was on Ecstasy.

I was sure this club would be the same. All gay clubs I'd been to had a meat-markety vibe. We were always on display. One needs to attract a potential mate, and that means perfect body, perfect face, perfect clothes, perfect skin, perfect smile, perfect hair, perfect everything. Or at least have three perfect things. Meanwhile, I'd given up on fixing my Klingon teeth.

Imagine that: a gay, feminine Klingon. I'd perhaps be called *baktag*, *todsah*, or some other forms of insult. When other Klingons train with their *bat'leth* sword, I'd be daydreaming about sniffing the right hand of a tall, dark, gorgeous senior warrior and fingering every curve of his sexy forehead ridges. I'd die without honor and be condemned to spend the afterlife in *Gre'thor*. Or, with my teeth and fondness for shiny things, I could be an Orc; a dainty one who'd lift his pinky while wielding a battle axe and prancing around in Bilbo's *mithril* shirt three sizes too small.

More people came in. I was surrounded. I should've planned ahead. I couldn't see the stage. I had hoped I could take photos. I couldn't tell if a Caucasian was smiling at me, cigarette dangling between his fingers.

People could smoke inside clubs in Indonesia. I always needed to wash my hair every time I went home from clubbing. I remember going to a club one night. I was barely inside for ten minutes but the cigarette smoke had already burned my eyes.

I ignored the Caucasian. "I'm on official business," I wanted to say. "I'm here for research. Absolutely not for pleasure."

An Indonesian stood next to me with his friend. He started swaying his shy, short, tubby body to a gaudy dance remix of "Call Me Maybe." His shoes caught my attention. Oh, my whiskers. They were studded loafers. The studs reflected the green dance floor lasers. He paired them with a studded wristlet. I could make out the ubiquitous monogram embossed all over it. I had no idea Louis Vuitton made studded wristlets. I looked around. Apparently, loafers were in. Black, gray, olive. Suede, leather, pleather. Matte, regular, patent. Plain, patterned, studded. I didn't own a pair of loafers and probably never would.

I'd spent three hours choosing my outfit. I ended up with what I always wore practically everywhere: black shirt, black jeans, black pleather Doc Martens boots. I wore my heavy silver jewelry and my fake septum ring. I wore my black eyeliner, black eyeshadow, black mascara, and rose-colored lip gloss. My look screamed, I am alternative, I am punk, I am goth, I am Iris Apfel lite. I blend genders. I am a black peacock. Why is no one buying me a drink?

I never had to dress up when I went to straight clubs. I was already special. I stood apart from gaggles of bland heterosexuals. If no one hit on me, I'd chalk it up to them being straight. Gay clubs were always another thing. I had to stand out, and if I couldn't be the cutest, I aimed to be the most bizarre. But maybe I was too strange. Or not enough. Maybe I should've worn studded loafers?

People around me were having fun. I started thinking, is anyone else alone? Is anyone else here for "research purposes"? Will I run into an old friend? Will someone talk to me? Will I get lucky tonight?

Three muscular go-go boys in matching tight chartreuse short shorts climbed onto the bar. In front of them, a group of people were celebrating someone's birthday. It was a woman's. The go-go dancers hoisted her up onto the bar. Their oily muscular bodies rubbed against hers. She stuffed bills into their tight briefs. Her friends' shrieks and laughter overpowered the assaulting music. ("We're not really claiming ourselves to be a gay club," the manager said. "Yes, we have gay patrons, but we also have straight women coming in and sometimes they take their boyfriends or their husbands.")

There goes the gayborhood.

I hated my skinny arms. I hated my skinny ass. I wished I could twerk. I wished I were up there, adored, desired, wanted. But no one wanted me there. No one wanted this stick insect dressed in all black.

The music changed. A dance remix of one of Katy Perry's songs. A young Indonesian man leaned back against another Indonesian man. He closed his eyes and smiled. The man behind him nuzzled his ear.

I was flooded with memories of walking hand in hand with The Pilot in the Castro. How freely we kissed while waiting for the train. Another box of memories opened and I was with The Baker at a mall in Jakarta. I was longing to hold his hand in public. I was mad that a boy and a girl walking in front of us could freely lip kiss, their arms around one another while we could only do that in the darkness of movie theaters, disentangling our arms as soon as the end credits started to roll, before the lights turned on.

The choppy song faded into the background as I watched the couple. Green laser beams doused the dance floor and lit the two men's faces. They looked so content, so free. And I got it. For a moment, I was not in Indonesia. I was in broad daylight in the street of the Castro, West Hollywood, London, Paris, Amsterdam, places where public display of gay affection is accepted. I got it. This was bigger than I was, bigger than my selfish, fearful self-loathing.

In a country where queers still live in a hush-hush condition, gay clubs are one of the few places where we can comfortably show our sexuality. These are safe havens, little pockets with no pressure from religions and heterosexual norms, and everything else that's considered "normal" in this country.

The music changed again. Heavy percussion. Samba. Tall feathered headdresses wove their way onto the stage from the front doors. Scattered spotlights hit the performers in crimson, blue, tangerine, white, and gold. Feather boas trailed behind them. The show was starting and I took my camera out of my bag. Back to work. I looked at the couple one last time and secretly basked in their joy.

JEALOUSY

"How do you deal with jealousy?" Ario asked.

"What do you mean?" I asked.

"Sometimes I don't like going out with my husband because he turns his head and makes sounds whenever he sees a cute guy. And please don't tell me that's what men do because I don't do that."

"You're a painter," I said. "When you see something visually appealing to you, don't you want to look at it as long as possible?"

"Yes."

"And don't you also make approving sounds?"

"Yes," he said, "but the painting at my house can't get jealous. Why are you defending this behavior?"

"It's okay to be jealous. It means you still love that person. It means you still care."

"I'm not talking about being jealous. I'm talking about inconsiderate spouses who make their partners jealous, whether or not they realize it."

I told Ario that near the end of my relationship with The Baker, I'd stopped pretending that I wasn't looking at other men whenever we were hanging out. He was always so upset but I couldn't stop myself.

"You're a dick," Ario said. "I hope you don't do it anymore."

"We're all attracted to beauty. We're all magpies. We're all sad little fishies that get hypnotized by the anglerfish."

"Those sad little fishies get eaten."

"You're right," I said.

He scoffed. "I knew it. You don't believe in the things you just said, do you? About that beauty bollocks?"

I told Ario about the time I was in Bali with my girlfriends. I was about twenty-one. We were going to get dinner when I walked past a fast food restaurant. In it was an older Caucasian gentleman with an Indonesian boy, maybe my age, maybe younger. They were talking and suddenly the older man stopped and looked at me and smiled. His Indonesian companion looked like he'd wanted to kill me, but I felt good.

"It felt good to have that kind of power," I said.

"Did it never occur to you how that boy must've felt?"

"It did," I said.

"Good," Ario said. "I'd probably stop talking to you if you didn't feel any remorse."

"I'm not a psychopath."

"You could be a sociopath. Anyway, I understand that we're all drawn to nice things. But you could try to be a little more discreet about it, especially in front of your husband. That's what marriage is. You respect each other's feelings. I don't know about you, but when my husband looks at other boys, I feel ugly. Inadequate. And I know you feel it too, so don't give me that 'we all look at pretty things' speech if you yourself don't believe that."

"You can't control what others think or do," I said.

"I guess not," he said.

NONIMMIGRANT VISA

APPLICATION CHECKLIST

- Printout of appointment confirmation page

- Passport (must be valid for six months beyond initial entry into the US)

- Receipt from an American-Embassy-appointed bank for payment for each visa applicant's fee ($160 for students)

- Printout of DS-160 confirmation page; must be printed on letter or A4 paper in portrait format

- One front-view, color 5cm x 5cm digital image photograph with a white background; photo should be taken within the last six months

- Original I-20 (for students)

- Criminal/court records pertaining to any arrest or conviction anywhere, even if sentence was completed or applicant was pardoned

- Original proof of income, pay slips, tax payments, property or business ownership, or assets, such as bank books, bank statements or certificates of deposit

AT THE EMBASSY

The American Embassy in Jakarta was probably the most heavily guarded compound in the city. Barricades of concrete steel blocks stood to the hip of the armed guards who patrolled the complex. One day, when I drove past it, I saw a military tank and rolled my eyes.

But that Monday, I was at the Embassy, fresh-faced and all smiles. My mother had woken me up an hour before, never mind that the Embassy was only seven minutes from where we lived. It was a few minutes before opening time and some people were already queuing for visas. I was still high from the success of my dance company's annual year-end recital on Saturday night. I'd written the show, designed the promotional materials, drafted the press release, and starred as the Grim Reaper, blindfolded with a scimitar balanced on my head.

The sixteen-foot steel gates were opened and people started walking in. A security guard directed our path and told us to turn off our cell phones and keep them away at all times.

"Next," the clerk at the check-in waved me forward. She was behind a glass window. I felt the air-conditioned breeze blowing from the square opening through which I slid the required documents. She looked at my nails. They were painted black. "A man with nail polish?"

I didn't detect hostility in her voice, and even if I had, I would've still displayed an impossible politeness. "Let those people have their way," my mother had told me.

"Oh, these were for a show," I said.

"What show?"

"A dance show last Saturday." I named the venue to make sure that she understood I was a legitimate performer. After all, we did perform at a sought-after, prestigious auditorium that had hosted local and international art shows since 1821.

The clerk nodded while scanning through my papers, passport, and photos, making sure I'd brought everything needed so that I wouldn't waste anyone's time. "You're good to go," she said and waved at the security guard in black who escorted me inside the building.

It wasn't long before my number was called and I was directed to another glass window.

"*Selamat pagi, apa kabar*?" a Caucasian woman smiled. I always feel a mixture of dissonance and pride when I see someone who's clearly not Indonesian speaks my language perfectly, albeit too formally.

"Good, thanks," I said in Indonesian and slid the documents through the opening. The woman didn't say anything about my nails.

"Going to the US to study?" she'd switched to English after skimming through my documents.

"Yes."

"What do you want to study?"

"I'm planning to get an MFA in creative writing and study belly dance."

"Belly dance? In the US?"

"Yes. The style I'm interested in is called American Tribal Style belly dance and it originated in San Francisco. The woman who developed it lives there and I'd like to learn from her and her troupe."

"Must be fun," she said. She sounded sincere. "But you're coming back to Indonesia, right?"

I thought of The Baker. We'd almost hit the two-year mark. I thought of my family and friends and cats. Of course I would come back. Just two years of grad school, then I'd return. Teach writing. Teach dance. Be a good son, friend, boyfriend, teacher, cat guardian, citizen. I told everybody this every time I was asked if I would come back.

"Definitely," I said. My nods were a bit too enthusiastic. My smile a bit too wide.

The woman leaned forward and put her face near the glass window like a schoolgirl who couldn't wait to share a juicy piece of gossip, and slowly said, "Beware of strange people. Find good friends. Take care of yourself."

"I will, thank you."

"Your visa will be ready in two weeks." She settled back into her chair and printed me a receipt. "Good luck and I can't wait to read your book."

She trusted that I was good enough to go to the US. She trusted that I wasn't a terrorist although I have an Islamic middle name courtesy of my mother. Maybe she realized that the only bomb I'd be carrying would explode in pink and rainbow glitter. And Muslims can't pray with nail polish on.

I was in and out in thirty minutes. Even my mother couldn't believe how fast it was. Now we could go shopping for clothes, and then I would meet The Baker for dinner and a movie. He took some time off work and had flown from Bali to Jakarta to spend my last days with me before I flew to the US.

THE DEMONS OF INDONESIA #2:

RADICAL MUSLIMS

Front Pembela Islam (Islamic Defenders Front) or FPI is a rogue terrorist organization. Think of it as the Westboro Baptist Church, only with more supporters and a more sophisticated system. And unlike the US, with its Bible Belt mostly in the Deep South, Indonesia is one big Qur'an Corset. FPI first became an unlikely hero in 1998 after defending an attack on a mosque in Jakarta. FPI and people from the neighborhood reportedly defeated about six hundred assailants who allegedly came from eastern Indonesia, where the majority of people are Christians (my father's family was from eastern Indonesia).

Soon after, true to its name, FPI appointed itself the moral compass of people and began sweeping, raiding, and closing down bars, clubs, and even street vendors selling food and drink during Ramadhan, the Muslim fasting month. The organization ambushed transgender gatherings at least three times. The most recent one was in 2010 in Depok, a city about forty minutes from Jakarta. Trans activists claimed that members of the FPI not only broke glassware but also assaulted a National Commission on Human Rights staff member who was present at the event as the local police department did nothing, proof that this terrorist group also has its claws deep in the flesh of the corrupt police force.

And now, FPI is still present and has more spinoffs than The Duggars' *19 Kids and Counting*.

A 2012 survey by private surveyor and political consultancy institution, Lingkaran Survei Indonesia, revealed that 80.6% of Indonesians do not wish to have gay neighbors. This number is way above the other two groups that Indonesians don't want to have as neighbors: the Shia (41.8%) and the Ahmadiyya (46.6%). Shia and Ahmadiyya are declared un-Islamic by Majelis Ulama Indonesia (Indonesian Ulema Council) or MUI. This council acts as a bridge between Islam and the supposedly secular government. It gives halal certification to products, claiming that small businesses with not enough capital can get it for free, while medium to large businesses pay between about USD 17 and USD 260. MUI is a private organization and it releases around four thousand halal certifications every year. It's interesting to note that FPI is also a member of MUI.

In March of 2015, MUI issued a *fatwa* (religious ruling) asking for a death sentence for gays on the grounds that homosexuality is a "vile act that is punishable by the death penalty," as well as a "deviant behavior that creates a stain on the dignity of Indonesia." Yet perhaps the most terrifying statement was, "it doesn't matter that they love each other."

YOUR DADDY'S RICH AND YOUR MA'S GOOD LOOKIN'

Listen, you really should see this, the mother says, but the son has already wandered off in the women's section of the store. She lets go of the thick woolen coat. The mother sees the son touch the sleeve of a woman's jacket. The son is smiling.

It's beautiful, the mother says. The son nods.

But it's not going to be warm enough. Here, this one should do it, the mother says. The son nods.

The black coat was made in Turkey and made its way to Indonesia. It's now purchased by a mother whose son is going to leave her to go to school in a country an ocean away.

They shared an understanding of fabrics. The mother kept a sewing machine in the son's room back in their old, two-story house. The son's room was the tiniest room, but then again, he is the youngest child. His parents' room in the old house was the biggest bedroom, the second biggest was his big sister's, then his older brother's. The son didn't have many things to keep in the floor-to-ceiling wardrobe, so the mother used some of the space to store curtains, linens, and the fabrics she'd bought that she hoped to one day turn into a pair of pants, or a shirt, or a dress.

The son saw the mother sew.

Teach me, the son said.

There were two different spools of thread. The bigger, taller one stayed upright far above, then the thread of that spool went down, through this loop and that loop until it finally reached down and looped into the needle. The smaller spool stayed hidden in a steel compartment that clicked safely shut, and the little wick of the thread was exposed just enough. The threads from the two different spools would meet and sew the fabric tightly.

See? the mother said. The son nodded.

When they moved into a new house in a better part of Jakarta twelve years later, and the son had a bigger room—one of the biggest bedrooms in the one-story house—they'd keep the sewing machine in his room.

✦✦✦

Listen, you really should see this, the mother says, but the son has already wandered off into the t-shirt section of the store. She lets go of the grey mullet cap with faux-fur earmuffs. The mother sees the son touch the sleeve of a black shirt. The son is smiling.

It's beautiful, the mother says. The son nods.

But that's not what we're here for. Here, what do you think of this one? the mother says. The son nods.

The cap was made in China and made its way to Indonesia. It being sold in tropical Jakarta makes no sense whatsoever, but the son will take it to San Francisco and Berkeley and Moraga, where it will keep his ears and head warm in the rainy and windy weather, where he will write stories about talking cats, four oddball cousins who must fight a demonic presence that has threatened their family for generations, a jilted lover who drives around in a stolen car with his boyfriend's bludgeoned body in the back seat, an estranged gay couple facing alien invasion, drag queens and their sexuality, drag queens and his sexuality, his lovers, his home country, and eventually the mother, but she will not understand these stories because she does not speak the language they will be written in.

✦ ✦ ✦

The son was four years old. He was silent.

The mother was forty. She was watching her son.

It was Saturday afternoon. They were in the car.

His teacher had scolded him for not following her order. She'd told him that he should only color one page of illustration for his homework. He'd colored the whole book. He was so happy when he was coloring them in front of the television, surrounded by his mother, his father, his sister, his brother. He'd misheard the instructions. He didn't know English. Or perhaps he hadn't understood what the teacher said even as she'd said it in Indonesian. They were his first lashes of pain, humiliation, and feeling of incapability that would mutilate and cripple him from time to time.

Before the son was born, before the son's older brother was born, the mother and the father had traveled to the US with their daughter to get his MBA from an Ivy League university in Boston.

The mother would smile every time she told the son the story about how difficult it was for her to explain to the store manager that she wanted peanut butter, to explain to the landlord that their heater wouldn't work, to explain to the doctor that their daughter had been sneezing and coughing.

But there they were, the mother and the son, in the car, on that Saturday afternoon.

Something wrong? the mother asked, not in Indonesian, but in English. The son nodded. He cried in her arms as he told her everything.

You don't have to keep taking lessons, she said, but if you do, it will take you places.

Now he also remembers how his mother uttered those simple words: in perfect English. The most perfect he'd ever heard his entire life.

✦✦✦

What did your friends say? the mother asks. They're at the mall's food court sitting down and snacking. The shopping bags occupy the third seat. Her bag and his purse occupy the fourth.

They asked me when I would be coming back, the son says.

Then what did you say?

I told them I'd come back in June. Then they laughed and said they thought I'd be gone for years.

What did your boyfriend say?

It's a good change for us. I mean, we're already in a long distance relationship anyway, what with him being in Bali and all. Now he can focus more on his job and I'll visit him in Bali when I'm here.

I like your boyfriend. I think he's a good person, the mother says. The son nods.

✦✦✦

The son was five or six. He was bored.

The mother was forty-one or forty-two. She was reading a magazine or a book.

They were in the car, in front of a Methodist church near their old house in Jakarta. They went to this church every Sunday. As a matter of fact, all the children were baptized at this church. Now the mother and the son were waiting for her husband, his father, to come out. He donated his time to audit the church's bookkeeping.

Dad is taking a long time, the son said.

Let's play a game, the mother put the magazine or the book down. The son nodded.

The mother took a small blanket from a compartment. She spread it and covered the son with it. The son giggled. You're a chick, she said. In an egg, all warm and safe.

The son saw the silhouette of the mother through the worn blanket.

The mother told him that he had to wait twenty-one days to come out of the egg. But for this, we'll just count to twenty-one, the mother said. The son nodded.

When they reached the number, the mother told the son that it was time to wake up, to stretch his tiny wing arms until the blanket fell around him, like soft eggshells.

The golden afternoon sun filtered its way in through the tinted car windows and the son squinted as he opened his eyes and saw his mother.

They played the game five more times, and each time the son hatched out of his blanket shell, she'd kiss his forehead and his cheeks and tell him that he was hers forever.

✦✦✦

I'll see you in six months, the mother says. The son nods.

People are around them. Preoccupied with their own farewells. Suitcases after suitcases.

You have everything? the mother asks. The son nods.

Passport, boarding pass, student visa, I-20, acceptance letter, insurance card. A new Samsonite suitcase, greenish beige. The son cringed at the color, but his mother had bought it for him. He was no longer a teenager. He was no longer ashamed to be seen with his mother. He'd grown to love her, to love the way she paired an "I Love Jogjakarta" shirt with baby blue grandma jeans and a colorful LeSportsac purse.

The son expects the mother to say something.

The mother doesn't say anything else, but the son still nods. The son, now taller than his small, Asian mother, bends forward to hold her.

She has rehearsed this. This routine, a choreography embedded deep in their muscle memories. It will repeat every time the son comes home at the end of every semester and flies away again before the beginning of every semester, enduring twenty-two hours of economy flights and transits each way, until even the greenish beige Samsonite breaks down.

The mother yearns for the day when it will all end, when the son comes back to her, stays with her, loves her until she passes.

The mother doesn't expect the son to break up with his Indonesian boyfriend, to fall in love with a musician, who loves the son so much that he'll fly to Indonesia to meet the mother and the father and the sister and the brother. A musician who promises a better life for her son although the mother has given the son the best years of her life and ultimately the best years of the son's life. But she sees the son smiling when he holds this man's hand in front of her.

She sees that the son is smitten by this man, that the son also loves this man, and she can't say, He's a wonderful man, but I want you to stay with me. Instead she will be the one who nods. She will tell the son how much she loves him and she wishes him the best, even though it means they won't celebrate his birthdays together, or her birthdays together. Even though it means long-distance phone calls will have to do. Even though it means she has to learn how to use emails, how to use Skype and WhatsApp, and how to manage living a life an ocean away.

BLACK SHAWL

The Baker bought me a shawl. This was in December, a month before my life in the US began. This was two years into our relationship, when we were in love, or when I had successfully made myself believe I was in love with The Baker.

My mother and I had forgotten to get a shawl during our shopping excursion. Meanwhile, we were told that San Francisco would have some cold days and cold nights. So the next day, The Baker and I went to a mall and he found a black shawl. It was a simple shawl. Black polyester and spandex blend. Spread it open and it would become a small cape. Fold it a few times and it was a scarf. I loved it and took it to the cashier. But The Baker took it from my hand and told me that it would be his gift.

The shawl stayed with me for three years. It warmed me through the Bay Area rain and wind. It stayed with me until one day I lost it on the bus in San Francisco when I was going out for a date.

GENTLEMEN SUITE: THE BAKER

Origin Story

Everyone loves an origin story. You introduce a character and people ask, "But what's his deal?"

The truth is I don't really know The Baker. You'd think that being in a relationship with someone for four years means you'd know everything about him.

I'd been to his parents' house in a neighborhood called Bekasi, a factory town about ninety minutes away from Jakarta. Whenever he was in Jakarta, and that was usually to visit me, he would stay at his parents' house there. It was an old, two-story building. Both his parents were in the military and he was an only child.

The Baker and I went to the same university, same campus, same faculty, but different majors, and he went to a good high school that had rejected me.

A few years before The Baker and I started a relationship, he'd gone through a difficult breakup and migrated from Jakarta to Bali. "To get away from it all," he said. He bummed around Bali for a while, doing odd jobs to support himself, before he was finally hired by a local textile company to act as a liaison to foreign fashion houses that wanted to outsource materials and workers for their products. One of his clients, an Australian prêt-à-porter company that specialized in women's apparel and accessories, loved him. He was later hijacked and worked exclusively for the company.

I came in as he was transitioning from being an office worker to working on his own for this Australian company. This was in early April of 2009. I'd been single for about three years and was filling the void with meaningless flings and casual encounters. He sent me a message on a gay dating site. His stats looked good (he was taller and not skinny), and things went really fast from there.

He flew to Jakarta in late April. After he took me out to a nice dinner at a fancy place, he asked me if I would want to be his boyfriend. He'd proven himself to be a polite and attentive gentleman (as promised, he'd turned off his Black-Berry during dinner).

I told myself, this is someone whom you can depend on, someone who won't cheat on you, someone funny and patient and understanding, someone who will keep his promise, someone who loves you very much. I told myself, you can easily forgive his flaws, such as his imperfect English and the fact that you don't find him attractive. It's not like you're the most perfect person in the world either.

Find someone who loves you more than you love him, they say. Even at that time, even as a narcissist, it didn't feel right to me.

But I said yes. Yes, I would very much like to be your boyfriend.

That same week, while he was in Jakarta, we opened a joint bank account. I had an awkward but otherwise pleasant dinner with his parents, and we drove to a city on the edge of the mountains three hours away for a honeymoon.

Details

As I was writing the chapters on The Baker, I found myself unable to remember details like our anniversary date, the name of the hotel we went to for our little getaway, or even the year of his birth. He blocked me on Facebook, and I could only rely on information from my own page, scrolling down through the years, finding cringe-inducing statuses of my younger, much stupider self.

This inability to remember can only be attributed to one thing, and not because it happened a long time ago. It's because it wasn't memorable. I took it for granted because I thought the chunk of it was not worth keeping. I remember fragments, sure, like the candlelit dinners and my trips to Bali where he took me to a restaurant in Ubud for the most delicious cinnamon bun. Like the time we went to a Sharia bank because it was the only bank that would let us open a personal joint account, although neither of us is a Muslim. But for the rest, I relied on photos that I uploaded to my social media accounts.

Our relationship is not memorable enough to make me think of him each time I devour a warm cinnamon bun (and that happens a lot). It's not memorable enough to make me think of him each time I see *Coraline* (we'd declared it our movie). It's not memorable enough to make me think of him each time I catch a glance of the tattoo on my back that I got in Bali (it was The Baker who researched the place, it was The Baker who patiently cleaned the wound and applied burn ointment on it for six consecutive days while I was staying at his place there). I do think of him whenever I pass by the coffee shop where I had talks with him about breaking up two days before New Year (we sat under a mural of a Turkish proverb that said coffee should be black as hell, strong as death, and sweet as love), or whenever I pass by the Chinese restaurant where we actually broke up the following month. But it is always a short thought, as short as his name. All the four years with him were condensed into two syllables of his first name that I could pronounce in half a second.

The memories of the last days of our relationship, on the other hand, were so vivid that they felt cartoonish, Technicolor fake, but they were the only strong memories I have of my time with him.

The Climb

Wait for me, he called to The Baker. But The Baker was already way up there. He couldn't even see him anymore. Hidden by the fog. He couldn't even hear the sound of pitons being hammered. He tugged on the climbing rope. It still felt secure, so he hoisted himself up again.

After a few yards of vertical climb, he saw The Baker, grinning and using the rope as a swing. Try to keep up, The Baker said, and started to climb again.

Wait, he said. You're going too fast.

Sorry, The Baker said, and slowed his pace.

He was grateful and he could catch his breath. After a while, The Baker returned to his old rhythm and climbed faster and faster and was out of sight once again.

Wait, he called after The Baker. Please wait. He climbed, but the rope somehow no longer felt secure. His muscles were tired, his breaths were short, and he was lightheaded.

He found a cave and thought The Baker was in there, but he got in and realized he was alone. The Baker was still farther up.

He wanted to care. He wanted to shout to him again to please wait. But he just stayed there. He didn't move. He sat bundled up so that whatever warmth he had left wouldn't escape. He had three options: he could rest for a while and resume climbing later, he could wait to see if The Baker noticed he was missing and hopefully he would come down and look for him, or he could just get off the mountain altogether and go get a nice cup of hot cocoa.

I'll Be Fine

"I can change," The Baker said. "I can slow down. We don't have to be engaged if that's what you want. We don't have to go look for a ring."

My dark hands looked dull and green against the white plastic table of the Chinese restaurant. I sipped my drink. It was drizzling and humid outside. January in Jakarta.

But I thought this had been going on long enough. We were hurting both of us.

"No," I said. "I don't think we can continue this. You deserve someone who actually loves you."

"You do know that this means I'll be blocking you out of my life, right?"

I was fully aware of it. I did the same thing to people who dumped me, which is why I'm not friends with most of my exes.

We didn't hug or share a kiss when we parted ways in front of the restaurant. Part of it was because we were in Indonesia after all, and also because I didn't want to.

"Will you be all right?" I said.

"Yes. I'll be fine," he said.

Withdrawal

But I wasn't fine. I missed several turns and spent an extra thirty minutes trying to get home. I'd lost a friend, and losing a friend is much worse than losing a lover. The problem was he didn't want us to be just friends, and I understood and respected that.

The sadness was so overwhelming that I phoned him and asked to meet him again. We were back together in less than twenty-four hours, and we both seemed to have forgotten that I'd told him I didn't love him.

The Coffee Shop

"Let's open a coffee shop," you said. This was two years into our relationship, going on the third. As usual, you were the one who came up with ideas of things to do together. Just like when you proposed, when you wanted us to get a ring. It bothered me how my friends became your friends that easily while I was still struggling to be friends with yours.

"How do we go about doing it?" I asked.

You told me about your friend who owned a small restaurant in Bali. He would give you the second floor for free to run a coffee shop. The details were sketchy. You just needed to use some money from the joint account. We were chatting through Internet messenger. Balancing our love life with your work and my studies, finding the time to overcome the sixteen-hour difference between Bali and Berkeley.

"But there are millions of coffee shops in Bali."

"It's going to be different. Every cup of coffee is going to be handmade, not machine made, so it has its own personality."

You named it after Jamie Oliver's television series. You worshipped him—the way he cooked, the way he explained what food was. I didn't get his appeal at all.

And so began the journey of our coffee shop in Bali. It was doomed from the start. Half-baked. Our little baby that we ignored. A child of divorce parents. I didn't even fight for custody. It was mostly your money anyway.

You left it to rot after I left you. What happened to the

posters that I designed? To the walls that were painted yellow? To the bar seats that overlooked the street and the messy telephone and electrical lines? To the printer in the corner that you named Bob Marley because, "It loves to jam"?

Would I be too narcissistic if I were to say that you left it because of me? Because you couldn't stand the ghost memories of me sitting in one of the chairs, looking at you, smiling at you, taking photos of the coffee and the cakes, designing the website?

Or maybe it wasn't just because of me. Maybe you had a falling out with the owner of the building, your friend who gave you the space for free. Our little freebie baby. It was almost always empty.

I never liked coffee anyway.

But I Did Know You
I knew your full name. I knew that your favorite color was blue. I knew that you loved to cook. I knew that you loved coffee. I knew that you collected Starbucks mugs, which was why I got you the cherry blossom one from my trip to Kyoto. I knew you used to love dogs and hate cats before I came into your life, and now you have cats in your farmhouse near the mountains a few hours away from Jakarta. (Yes, I've been asking my friends—who became your friends— about you.)

I knew you were always there to help me, like that time my dance troupe and I were setting up our very first recital at that strange and dusty auditorium. You came and stayed with me to help put the screen up. And we kissed and fondled and almost had sex in the darkened auditorium, behind the curtains.

I knew you loved horror movies. You were a big fan of

the *Saw* series, especially the first film, and you never forced me to watch them with you. I was grateful for that.

I knew you loved my family, that you were ready to grow old with me and help me take care of my brother.

Don't Keep Fluttering Away
I was in Indonesia for the summer, doing research for my drag queen thesis. The Baker had accompanied me to Jogjakarta. He'd also booked the car and the driver and the hotel.

I'd also been invited to perform at a wedding in Bali, which was good for my thesis project because my client paid for the plane tickets. The Baker invited me to stay at his new place, which was good because then I didn't have to pay for a hotel. I found out later that the performance was five minutes away from his place. He rented a car and drove me around to see the people I wanted to interview and to the wedding gig.

You could say I used him. You could say I abused his devotion to me, his happiness to see me.

The Baker and I were lying on his bed. We just had sex. Or he just had sex while I lay under him like roadkill. I didn't even let him kiss me. I let him fuck me just because I couldn't bear to suck his penis. He came shortly after, and I was glad it was over.

His ginger cat meowed in the living room, demanding to be let in. He meowed for a while before he found something else to do.

"This needs to stop," I said.

The Baker held me. I lay still under him. "Don't say it," he said. "Don't say the word."

In January, I'd taken the word back, but I couldn't be any more certain now. The Pilot was waiting for my return, and I couldn't wait to be with him.

"When are you going to settle down? You can't keep fluttering away. You can't leave every time someone better comes along."

The air in the room was dead. We didn't turn on the air conditioner, but the marble floors kept the room several degrees below the outside temperature. The white bed sheet with pictures of blue boats was itchy and felt coarse on my skin. The ginger cat began meowing again.

I broke free and went to the bathroom. A few months later, when I was back in Berkeley, I decided to cut off all communication from him, and unfriended him on Facebook—a fate that The Pilot would share not long after.

The Biggest Bitch of All

"But Darling," Ario said, "you do know you're the bitch in this relationship, don't you?"

"Geez," I said. "Are you my Jiminy Cricket now?"

"Well, I'm not the one who dumped his boyfriend of four years, the man who'd loved him, who'd put up with him, for someone else."

"Yes. All right. Fine. I take full responsibility for my actions. But you should know that he was also stifling me. Can't you understand that?"

"What I wouldn't give for a man as devoted as that."

"You can have him," I said.

"Do you have his photo?"

I shook my head.

Ario laughed. "Just say it."

"Say what?"

"Admit that you think he's a minger," Ario said. "That you're ashamed of him. That you don't even want to show his photograph to me."

"Isn't that a bit too harsh?" I said. "Even for you?"

"Apparently not for you."

"Do you have any idea how abrasive you're being right now?"

Ario laughed again, but he realized he had offended me, so he pulled a classic Ario, where he made you think he was apologizing, but not really.

"I'm sorry," he said, "but you know how I feel about cheaters."

"Excuse me? Need I remind you that you also destroyed someone else's relationship?"

Ario looked at me as though I had just kicked a puppy. He took a slow suck on his cigarette. The embers ate away at the thin paper as the tobacco turned to ashes.

"You're right," a mist of cigarette smoke escaped his mouth. "You're right. Of course. My God, we're all bitches, aren't we?"

"Not as big of a bitch as karma," I said.

"Ah yes," Ario said. "That one is the biggest bitch of all."

DISTRACTIONS

Ario's parents were fighting again. They were about to leave for his school's Christmas party. He was nine years old. His mother had accused his father of sleeping with one of his assistants. She'd flung his files and papers off the table. That was the first and only time he ever saw his mother become violent when she was angry with his father. He thought she would be spiteful all night, but at the party, his mother was like someone else. She mingled with her friends. She laughed and helped set up the food and drinks. She clapped when the little ones opened their presents.

"She was unaware that I was watching her," Ario said.

"Because you were embarrassed?" I said.

"No, quite the opposite. I wanted her to have a good time. I didn't want her to be sullen and unhappy. I felt I was partially responsible for that."

"Why?"

"Well, if there hadn't been a Christmas party, we wouldn't have needed to go. And she could've had more time to deal with my dad."

"But distractions are good, right?" I said.

"That's what I thought."

The next morning, little Ario caught a fever. It was the rainy season after all. His mother took him to the family's pediatrician, but the visit wasn't all about him.

"My mom told the pediatrician, 'I've been having trouble sleeping lately.'"

The pediatrician gave her a look that said, "Why are you telling me that?" but he asked her some questions anyway and they came home with Ario's cold lozenges and her sleeping pills.

The next morning, when his parents were gone and he stayed at home because he was sick, he went to his mother's room and searched for the pills. She was one of those people who kept keys in secret places. Ario had already been in a lot of trouble for opening locked drawers, for snooping around, and finding his father's porn stash. His mother would spank him, lock him in the shed, but he couldn't stop. He was always curious. It took him a while to find the key because his mother had hidden it somewhere else, but little Ario found it. The pills were exactly where he thought they would be—stashed inside the locked closet drawer, behind envelopes of cash and his dead grandmother's gold jewelry.

But he knew he couldn't just throw away the pills or hide them. His mother would know. Luckily, the pills were those joined capsules that one could twist open and put together. So he did that. He twisted the capsules open one by one, dumped the white powder into the toilet, twisted them closed, and put the empty shells back inside the clear, plastic bottle. Two or three capsules were mangled when he twisted them too hard, but his mother wouldn't notice. He flushed the toilet, put the plastic bottle behind the cash and the jewelry, locked the drawer, placed the key back in its hiding place, and went back to his room to sleep.

"This whole thing, this whole business of suicide, I just don't get it. And I'm not saying that because I'm happy or content with my life. No. And I know I'm saying it and maybe in two weeks I'll change my mind and jump off the Pasadena bridge and be another number in the statistics. I just don't know what the appeal is. Freedom? But what's beyond death? We don't know. And I hate uncertainty."

"Promise to call me or text me or whatever when you feel the urge," I said.

"That's not the point. That's not what I want. My point is, my dad's infidelity almost drove my mom to the brink of suicide, and I'm a momma's boy. It's in our blood to be jealous, to be possessive. And I really, really can't take it anymore with my husband."

"But aren't jealousy and possessiveness normal in a relationship?"

"That's what I thought too," Ario said. "Apparently people here have this weird understanding about marriages and open relationships. Meanwhile, I'm happy to be Asian and have Eastern values."

"Why don't you have sex with someone else?"

"Didn't you hear what I just said?"

"Don't get mad. Get even. Have sex with someone else. You're hot. You can have any man you want. I guarantee you'll feel better."

"Isn't that cheating?"

"You're already in an open relationship," I said. "Take advantage of that."

"Don't tell me you're also in an open relationship?" Ario said.

"That, my darling, is actually none of your business."

Ario scoffed. "Bloody Americans. There is no such thing as gay marriage in Indonesia. And even when I was there, I was always in a monogamous relationship. My boyfriends and I didn't even think of looking at other men. Now these people have all the privilege and it's still not enough for them. No. They want the marriage and its benefits and still want to fuck other people."

"That's human. We're never satisfied."

Ario looked at me as though I'd just said something incredibly stupid and offensive.

"I don't believe you. Are you sure you're Indonesian?"

"I can also be a liberal."

"You're right. It's your life anyway," he said. "All right. So, tell me, what hook-up apps do the cool and sexy kids use these days?"

21

A VISIT

When Ario was six or seven years old, he'd developed this habit of lying on his stomach with his feet up while doing whatever.

One time, it was on the marble floor of his grandmother's living room. He was tracing the embossed pattern of a diamond on a piece of paper, and then drawing peacocks with eyelashes on its side. It was his fifth attempt and it always ended up the same way: either he couldn't get the pattern right or the peacocks would be too ugly.

His mother was somewhere else when his stout grandmother appeared in the living room. She was wearing a peach traditional women's top with lace embroideries in the front and a batik sarong.

"Don't lie on your stomach with your feet up," she said. "Otherwise your mother will die soon. It happened to me with my own mother."

Even today, whenever he's lying on his stomach, he still consciously tries not to put his feet up.

MATRIARCH

He dragged her, kicking and screaming, clawing and hissing, and put her inside the pink kitty carrier. She was the oldest and only female cat in the household of four felines. Now that he was home in Jakarta, he could finally drive her to the veterinarian, some thirty minutes away from where they lived.

She used to be plump, her grey-white tabby fur sleek and clean. Now she'd become lighter, her fur matted and dull. Her pink nose had turned brown. This frightened him. The thought of death, the thought of not being there to say goodbye. He had already suffered this when one of his tomcats died of a urinary tract infection and he was in Los Angeles with his husband, The Musician. The scarcity of news from home haunted him. When did the tom become sick? When did they start noticing that he no longer wanted to drink or eat? Was he euthanized or did he die because he let go?

There was no one to blame for the death. No one to blame for the neglect, except him. He was sure the people at the house (the two maids and his mother), had done everything they could to save him, to get him to the veterinarian as soon as possible, but not soon enough. Had he been there, he would've noticed. He would've had the time and the energy to bring him to the hospital. His mother was turning sixty-six and she no longer wanted to drive.

He was photographing a literary reading at a bookstore

when his mother sent the news. He shouldn't have checked his phone, but he was bored of a poet's piece (it bothered him too that poets seemed to have the worst stage presence—they never look at the audience) and he did what everyone in this century does when one's bored. He checked his phone and found the text. He looked for his husband in the bookstore who cradled his head as he cried. A minute later, he returned to his spot and resumed his duty.

He didn't want the same thing to happen to this cat. She was old. Eleven years and counting. Approximately sixty-five years old in human terms. He couldn't find her documents, but he found the ones that belonged to her sisters, who'd died years ago. Street accidents. Both of them. There was no one to blame for their deaths, and curiosity does kill cats, but he blamed his parents' decision to move them to this house in front of a busy street. Their old house was not in a neighborhood this affluent, but it was quiet and peaceful.

A decade ago, his first cat, who shared similar physical traits with this old cat, was ten years old when she died of cancer that had spread all over her body. When she was healthy, she used to jump on the bed and sleep by his foot, but she spent her final days under his bed. He could hear her short, shallow breaths. He didn't want to let her go. He wanted her to pass in her own time. But his mother convinced him otherwise.

His mother drove them to the veterinarian to put her to sleep. On the way, she died in his arms, as though not wanting him to bear the guilt. He buried her in the side courtyard in front of his room, placed flowers, poured perfumed water, and lit a candle for her. He didn't tell anyone, but her illness and death helped take his mind off his first heartbreak.

But the veterinarian declared this eleven-year-old

healthy. Quite possibly because she was spayed and never bore kittens. Great teeth. No fleas or ticks. Her kidneys had started to slow down, but that was expected of senior cats. Her fur had started to lose its shine, but that was also normal. He was allowed to give her a bath either in the morning or in the afternoon, when the sun was no longer harsh. A diet change was also strongly recommended. He would see to it.

This was good news. But he knew he wouldn't be there to grow old with her. He did abandon her. He would soon leave again and come back to his husband and the little house they shared with two cats. The best thing he could do was to make sure she would be given the proper food.

But how could she live this long? How could she still have the strength of younger felines? (He dreaded giving her a bath, what with those sharp claws.) Did her sisters give her their lives? He hoped they did. Imagine that. A cat inheriting the remaining life lengths of her two dead siblings.

He hoped to see her again the next time he came back to Jakarta. He hoped she would still remember him, even as the bitch who kidnapped her and placed her on the cold, steel table to have her poked and prodded.

YOUR FAULT

If my best friend hadn't stolen my boyfriend, I wouldn't have bought a gym membership. If I hadn't been a member of that gym, I wouldn't have learned to belly dance. If I hadn't learned to belly dance, I wouldn't have known what American Tribal Style belly dance was. If I hadn't learned American Tribal Style belly dance, I wouldn't have wanted to go to San Francisco.

I learned about Sylvia Plath because I was always interested in suicides. I found *The Bell Jar* because I learned about Sylvia Plath. I decided to become a writer after reading *The Bell Jar*. I was able to read *The Bell Jar* because I could speak, read, and write English. I could speak, read, and write English because my parents forced me to learn it ever since I was young.

I wonder if my parents realize that if they hadn't made me learn English, I would've never left them.

If my relationship with The Baker hadn't been a disaster, I wouldn't have met The Pilot, and then I wouldn't have met The Musician.

But Annie Lennox wouldn't have happened if she hadn't left Eurythmics, Sylvia Plath wouldn't have made her best works if there hadn't been an affair, and Indonesia would've never gained its independence from the Japanese if the Japanese hadn't attacked Pearl Harbor and the US hadn't dropped atom bombs in Hiroshima and Nagasaki in revenge.

DIVA

The lady's fair face is bare. Clean. Scrutinized under dozens of egg-shaped bulbs that frame the mirror in front of her. Her black hair is short, practical, not in the way, and so is her black spaghetti-strap top. She brushes her eyebrows. Then she hesitates. Why? Why? She curls her eyelashes. She bites her thumb. She plays with a brush, circling it around her left eye, then the right. She tells herself too many times why she doesn't learn to keep her big mouth shut. She applies pink press-powder eye shadow with her fingers. She fills her eyebrows with the richness of dark brown. She lines her eyes with jet-black paint and widens her eyes to apply mascara onto her eyelashes.

She lets her highlights bake as she plays with dark magenta and tangerine feather boas. The colors match her eye makeup. She poses this way and that, tilting her head back, before ripping the boas away from her skin to resume painting her face. Why? Why? Her lips are now scarlet. Her eye shadows are now shimmering. Her head is now covered with a glittering tangerine headdress. Feather boas jut out of it and snake their ways down behind her. White rhinestone earrings dangle from her ears. A white rhinestone art deco necklace hangs around her neck. She caresses them with her hands, now hidden underneath black satin gloves. This boat is sinking and she's ready for her close-ups.

He only saw bits and pieces of the video when it first

came out in the '90s. But he saw the album's poster at a record store when he was a child. He couldn't stop staring at this creature. Those imposing, distant eyes, the jawline and nose line that were so different from his, so strong, and those feathers, those rhinestones, those cheekbones.

"We're late," his mother said as she softly took his little hand and pried him away from the spell.

"Mama," he said, "what's a 'diva?'"

His mother, who could barely speak English, didn't answer, and the question remained unsolved for years. He never learned who the person in the picture was. All he knew was that he wanted to be her, with feathers and red lips.

Years later, when he got ahold of the entirety of Annie Lennox's "Why" video, he had already developed a fascination for makeovers, for transformations. The incongruence of this showgirl, in all her regalia, posing demurely and looking detached and can't be bothered, intrigued him.

The showgirl lashes out. She says in a breathless rant that whoever she's talking to just doesn't get her tears, doesn't get her life, doesn't get her as a person.

His queer identity got her—but wait, there's more. She's a dancer, entertainer, someone who's supposed to make people laugh and forget about their regrets and disappointments, while she, and the audience, ignores her own regrets and disappointments.

And he thought of his mother. I'm sure she has regrets. I'm sure she has disappointments. But what kind of regrets? What kind of disappointments? Am I one of them? Am I two of them? Three? Eight? Thirty-eight? He thought of his mother. When he was six, she caught him applying her baby pink lipstick on his lips and her powder on his face once, and some days later she no longer wore lipstick and powder.

She caught him wearing her high heels once and then some days later those high heels disappeared from their house. He asked her about them and she said, "Oh, I gave them away. I couldn't walk in them." He was surprised because not only did he love wearing them, he could run in them, climb stairs in them, and he loved every clack the heels made every time they touched the floor.

His mother, she says she loves him and is proud of him, she shows him her love and her pride. But if only he could be in that silent, solitary room, when she cried after confirming all the tell-tale signs of his sexuality, when she murmured her why, why, and prayed to a force he no longer believed in. If only he could be there with her before she emerged out of the room as a showgirl, poised, professional, he would cry with her, but probably couldn't explain to her why he's this way because even until now, that question remains unsolved.

But he would tell her that now he knows the meaning of the word "diva," and that without a doubt, she is his diva.

LINEAGE

That night, when The Musician was asleep next to him, he thought of his silent mother, and the storm she had weathered when she decided to leave her family to be with his father. They'd faced their own share of scrutiny when he married her. His father was raised a Protestant, his mother a Muslim, but they went on with it anyway and have stayed married for more than forty years. To this day, many couples in Indonesia who don't worship the same religion are still facing pressures from their relatives and religious leaders to break up.

He thought of her father, a grandfather he never knew because he died when she was a child. He thought of her mother, a figure so loving and so old-fashioned, whose house in the sleepy city of Cirebon was a train ride four hours away from Jakarta—an eternity for a six-year-old. He remembered his grandmother's house, the house where his mother grew up with her brother. Everything seemed to be painted in sepia. Even its peculiar earthy smell and the big bed that his mother and his siblings would sleep on whenever they were there. The street's name was Happiness Alley. And he always insisted they catch the first train back to Jakarta before the morning *adhan* (riding two paddy cabs to the station, one for them and one for their suitcases), and because he was a selfish, spoiled child, he never thought of the conversations between his mother and her mother during those early hours.

Were they ever sad she left? Did her mother ever ask her to stay just one more night? Her older brother passed away too early, leaving a wife and three teenaged children. Her mother would too, a few years later. And the family she grew up with was gone and she was alone.

Now, lying beside the man that would be his husband, he was old enough to understand grief, to understand change and loss and loneliness. But regret always comes too late.

THE DEMONS OF INDONESIA #3:

TIFATUL SEMBIRING AND FAHIRA IDRIS

There will always be bigots. Unfortunately, in Indonesia, those bigots are in the congress. Some of them were even appointed ministers, such as Tifatul Sembiring, who came from a conservative Muslim party called Partai Keadilan Sejahtera (Prosperous Justice Party) or PKS. Ironically, he became the minister of communications and information technology. He claimed that pornography caused HIV and said that funding to fight the virus and disease was a waste of money. He tweeted that gays were the cause of natural disasters. Backed by then-president Susilo Bambang Yudhoyono (arguably the worst Indonesian president in history), he forced Indonesia back into an era of Internet censorship. But he was more interested in blocking porn sites than those that cater to radical Muslims. Sembiring ruled from 2009 until 2014.

Indonesia also has its own version of Sarah Palin. Her name is Fahira Idris. They both love guns and hunting. They're both religious fundamentalists of two different Abrahamic religions (Palin is Christian and Idris is Muslim). And they're both anti-gay.

Idris' rise to fame began in August of 2010 when she criticized Front Pembela Islam (Islamic Defenders Front) or FPI on Twitter after the terrorist group attacked a church in Bekasi, a city about forty minutes away from Jakarta. She then came to their office to talk with them face to face. People called her courageous and revolutionary. A month later, when FPI forced the shutdown of a gay film screening that was part of the annual Q! Film Festival at the Dutch cultural center in Jakarta, Idris stayed mum. In March of 2013, she tweeted that gays were predators that preyed on "children of the country" (literal translation of *anak bangsa*). It is unknown whether she was equating queers to pedophiles or if she was using the term "children" figuratively.

Still, for the tweet about FPI, she won The Most Inspiring Tweeter poll (71%, sixty points above the runner up, a consultant from Atlanta, GA). The poll was organized by TheTop10Blog.com, and Indonesians, ever so hungry for international achievements and recognitions, thought this was a huge thing and made Idris their hero. The image she projects is something that many Indonesians dream to be or to have—a successful entrepreneur, a religious woman wearing hijab, a wife and mother. In August of 2014, she used her power to successfully lobby for the recall of the Indonesian translation of *Puberty*, a children's educational comic book from the series of *Why?* by Korean Ji-eun Jeon. Idris criticized the book for pushing gay propaganda because there were panels that promoted tolerance of same-sex love and transfolk.

Still, the Global Peace Index, the panel that decides which countries are the most peaceful, ranks Indonesia #46 (out of 162). The US is #94 on that index. Because of guns.

SAVE THE DATE

"So," the lawyer said, "how did you two meet?"

Their documents were on his glass table. His spacious office was in one of those art-deco buildings in downtown Los Angeles. They were practicing questions and answers for the immigration interview.

"Through a mutual friend," The Sculptor said. "Late August?"

"Yes," Ario said. "You were visiting SoCal. You were on your way to a Napa Valley wine tour or something, and one of my professors is your friend."

"You had a few drinks, and then you were all over me," The Sculptor said.

"That's not true," Ario said. "I had one glass of wine. It was enough for me to be all over you."

"Was that when you both fell in love?" the lawyer asked.

They nodded.

"What did you see in each other?"

"He's funny. He makes me laugh a lot," The Sculptor said. "He's dependable. He's kind. Back in Berkeley, every time he bought dinner, whenever there were leftovers, he'd give it to a homeless person."

Ario couldn't believe he remembered that.

"See? I remember things too."

"And when did you get engaged?"

"On a really terrible day. It was a terrible day for me,"
The Sculptor said. "But he turned it around."

"Here in the US?"

"The day I gave you the painting."

"Here in the US?" the lawyer repeated.

"Yes, why?" Ario asked.

"And did you fly back to Indonesia afterward?"

"No, why?"

"You can't tell them you're engaged before you're back
in the US," the lawyer said.

"Why?" The Sculptor asked.

The lawyer looked at Ario. "You swore to return to Indonesia when you received your student visa. Being engaged
when you were in Indonesia means when you flew back to
the US, you knew you wouldn't return to your country."

Ario was still trying to understand that logic when The
Sculptor said, "No, it was here in the US. At my house in
Glendale. We danced to Edith Piaf. His favorite."

"When was this?"

"Valentine's Day weekend," Ario said. He remembered
it not because it took him a month to finish the mandala
painting, not because of the seven-hour shuttle ride when he
couldn't stop fidgeting because he was worried the tube that
contained the painting would get smushed. He remembered
because they had a big fight that weekend, that Valentine's
Day weekend. Not only did it almost destroy their relationship, it almost killed him.

"Sounds good. Use it when immigration asks you that
during the interview," their lawyer said. "Also, make an album or a scrapbook of your relationship so that they know
it's not a fraud."

EXCAVATION

My editor put it beautifully when I said I was having a painful time writing some of the chapters. She called it "excavating."

I imagine parts of my fossilized memories were stored under a vast desert land with a fleet of dirty and sweaty paleontologists in cargo shorts and boots, digging and chipping and brushing layers and layers of sand and earth and rock formations, being careful not to damage fossil records of even the tiniest creatures. How one found fossilized microscopic life forms is baffling to me. We always put importance on the big ones, especially those that are considered dangerous, with sharp teeth and claws, ready to rip and tear. We imagine how it would be if it were to terrorize a prehistoric park on a remote island, or what it would do if it were loose in a big city, thirsty and hungry and looking for its child. We like to scare ourselves. We get off on it.

HE THREW A MALLET

Ario was at The Sculptor's house when this happened. It was Valentine's Day weekend. Their first one together. The Sculptor was still in bed. Ario was still in love. The mandala painting was safely tucked back inside its tube. Ario was a little bit disappointed. He thought it would look perfect on The Sculptor's workshop room wall. He scanned the room. There was a table with a lump of clay, a steel shelf of nude figures, cardboard boxes containing God knows what, an oven, a shelf of metal tools. Ario wondered why The Sculptor had needed the shelf. There were tools everywhere. He decided that it would be a good idea to collect them. Spruce the place up a little bit. Make it more tolerable. Maybe The Sculptor would get inspired.

He began by picking the tools, classifying them based on usage. Scrapers, chippers, there were at least five chisels of same size. He found wires too. Some were in good condition, but some were tangled and rusty. He put them in a box. Wire cutters, X-Acto knives, some with exposed blades. Ario shook his head and rolled his eyes, but he was still smiling.

This guy's a mess, he thought, but it takes one to know one.

Ario's tiny apartment in Berkeley was just as cluttered. Putting things back after a project was the hardest part. Ever since he was a child, he was always the one who put the Christmas tree up. He'd leave the job of taking it apart in the capable hands of the maids. Now he was being domestic.

He moved on to the shelf. He thought he would dust

the shelf, but that would mean removing the statues. There were dozens of statues on the shelf. Headless with literally chiseled torsos. He wondered what it would take for him to have that kind of body. He never really liked the gym and never really thought it was necessary to go there. He loved walking, though. He found solace in every step. It helped him think.

The shelf had three levels and on the bottom were boxes. The one on the very left had an open top, unlike the rest. He slid it out. There were knick-knacks, unfinished sculptures, broken mugs and cups. Must be the rejects, Ario thought, but something gleamed under them. He carefully extracted it. It was a plate. Smooth china with gold rims. On it was a painting, shiny black and gold. Two faces. He recognized one face. It was The Sculptor's, but he didn't know who the other one was.

"Put it down," The Sculptor said. He was standing by the door. His sudden appearance shocked Ario and he dropped the plate.

It shattered under him.

The Sculptor cursed.

This was when Ario stopped his story. But he pointed at the floor in The Sculptor's workshop room and I saw a small area, about ten inches by ten inches, where it looked like someone had put a new plaster.

"This was where I stood that day," Ario said. "I didn't move after I dropped the plate."

The mark on the floor was several inches in front of Ario.

"That was where he threw the mallet."

"The what?"

Ario went to the tool shelf and took out a hammer. He handed it to me and I felt its weight.

"You could've been killed," I said.

Ario chuckled.

"Sometimes I wish he'd killed me that day."

"You have to get out of here," I said. "Get away from him."

"Oh, that was years ago," Ario said. "He hasn't done anything like that ever since."

"Aren't you worried that he may do it one day?"

Ario scoffed. "These days I've been invisible to him. He doesn't even look at me anymore when we're talking. If we're talking at all."

"Maybe you just need to go back to Jakarta. Take a few weeks, meet your family, your friends, then come back to Los Angeles."

"I can't."

"Why not?" I asked.

"Everyone will ask why I'm in Jakarta alone," Ario said. "Everyone will ask where my husband is."

"Tell them he's busy with work, but that he's still missing you and can't wait to go home. And by home, I mean here."

"What if he isn't?" Ario asked.

"Isn't what?"

"Isn't missing me? What if when I come back, I find him already in love with another man?"

"Then it's a good thing. Then you can leave him and won't have to live your life dreading when a mallet is going to actually hit you."

"But then I'll lose the chance of being a citizen."

"I thought you hated this country."

Ario didn't answer. He just lit another cigarette and took the mallet out of my hands. He left the story unfinished.

IT'S NOT AS EASY AS IT LOOKS

When you're an immigrant, and you moved to another country, and you have a fight with your husband, you can't just drop everything and say, "I'm going to my mother's."

And if you're lucky enough to have friends, you can't sleep at your friend's house because no matter how well you know them, no matter how close you are with them, you hope to work the issues out with your husband and you don't want things to get awkward when said friend invites the two of you for Christmas dinner.

You share that mansion, or that house, or that tiny apartment, where you bump into one another all the time and you can either talk it through and bury the hatchet, or go to war.

THE CHAMBER

Our memories are radioactive. They seep into objects and contaminate them, causing them to have identity crises so they no longer know if they are good or bad. But if we're lucky (and I believe most of us are), there's a special vault deep in the bunker of our memory library. Before we go in, we must decontaminate ourselves, shed our hazmat suit, store our gizmos that connect us to the world (there's no reception anyway), and leave our nonsense and pretense and our need to please or offend everyone, and walk in with the same kind of fearlessness that is made of callused trust that has been heated and forged and doused and tested a million times.

There is only one requirement for an object to be kept in this special vault: it must allow and help us stay in the present, whether it's a sad, joyful, chaotic, or serene present. It bars us from regretting the past or worrying about the future.

Some of us keep Adderall and poppers and a Bible in this vault. Some of us keep weed and a drawer full of spirits. Some of us keep a fridge perpetually stocked with Boston cheesecakes and cherry pies. Some of us keep vibrating dildos and lube. Some of us keep Blu-ray discs of *The Lord of the Rings* trilogy, extended version with director's commentary. Some of us keep Sufi poetry books and a Qur'an. Some of us keep a dinner and movie date with a best friend from school. Some of us keep a yoga mat. Some of us keep a razor or a pair of sewing scissors.

In my vault, I have two boxes. One contains my make-up kit. Brushes, eyeshadows, eyeliner, concealer, foundation, powder, highlighter, eyelash curler, mascara, tweezers, blush, the whole shebang. The other contains velvet fringe scarves to tie around my hips, four small brass cymbals to go around my fingers, and a handful of songs for me to dance to until I feel ready to put on my hazmat suit again and deal with life.

GENTLEMEN SUITE: THE PILOT

Flight Plan

"I'm not masculine," I said in a message to The Pilot. German genes. Great jaw. Great shape. He went to the gym five times a week. He didn't drink. He didn't smoke. Hazel eyes. A cross between Rob Brydon and Bruce Willis. Twenty years my senior.

"What do you mean?" he replied.

"I wear eyeliner and nail polish. And jewelry."

"Love it. So when can we meet?"

Taxi

The Pilot stood leaning against the railing at Castro Street Station. We shook hands. He was two inches shorter.

"You hungry?" The Pilot asked.

"Starving," I said. It was Saturday afternoon. We met after my dance class in The Mission.

"Good, let's go."

He took me to a Chinese restaurant a few blocks away from the gym he went to.

"You're vegetarian?" he asked.

I nodded. "You?"

"Nah."

"I don't mind," I said. "I'm not a veganazi."

"Good word. I should use that. That said, I'd rather see

some humans die than animals. There are billions of people and only what? A few thousand cheetahs?"

I smiled and said I agreed. We ordered vegetarian fried rice and a tofu dish.

"So, you're here on student visa?" The Pilot asked.

"Yes. I just started a new semester. My last year."

"Cool. Where?"

I told him where I went to school. I told him that it's Lasallian.

"Sounds religious," he said. "I hate organized religions. Nothing good ever comes out of them."

I told him that I was raised in a religious household, and that one time, out of the blue, a pastor gave a sermon and told everyone that gay people would go to hell. The Pilot rolled his eyes, but he didn't say a word. He let me unload on him. This strange boy with so much baggage, but he didn't trivialize it. He listened.

"You're with me now," he said. "You don't need to be afraid of clergymen telling you that you'll go to hell."

I believed him.

Take Off

We were waiting for MUNI on Church Street Station to take us back to his house near Ocean Beach.

"Thank you for lunch," I said.

"Thank you for accompanying me," he said.

I wish I remembered what prompted me to lunge forward and kiss him. I wish I had written it down somewhere. On a piece of paper. On my palm. In my brain. In my heart. All I could remember was bending my knees and we kissed.

It must've felt good because I ended up in his bed in his

blue bedroom in his spotless house, surrounded by model airplanes. We had sex under a little ceramic plaque with a plane and the words that said, "Flying is the second greatest thrill known to man and landing is the first."

"You smell so nice, so clean," The Pilot said. He hit all the right buttons when he made me cum the first time we had sex. No one had ever done that, and no one probably will. My orgasm was a nice change. About time too. Spring was just starting.

Cruise

The Castro soon became my home. The Pilot and I walked hand in hand whenever he was in town and not on flying assignments. I'd meet him at his gym and we'd head out for dinner, or we'd meet in downtown and watch a movie, or I'd go straight to his house and we'd have a weekend in, just lying naked in bed doing movie marathons. Our favorites were *The Lord of the Rings* and *Alien* saga.

It was a month after we'd been seeing each other. He was in bed. I just got out of the shower. We had gone to Chinatown earlier and I couldn't stop staring at an enameled pewter ring holder in the shape of a peacock.

"Come here," he said. We kissed. He licked his lips. "Fresh and minty."

"I brushed my teeth."

"I can tell." He kissed me again, but he broke off and got off the bed. "Don't go anywhere."

I took off the blue bathrobe that he'd let me use and knelt naked on the bed. It was grey outside. The ocean was a few blocks away and I could almost see it through his bedroom window. I smiled when I heard him whistle and felt his lips on the small of my back.

"For you," he said.

It was the key to his house.

He fucked me hard that evening, and as he came, he told me he loved me.

Flight Path

"Take the L-train," The Pilot said. "L for losers."

"L for luuuv," I kissed him. He smiled.

"It's quite a ride, but once you get to Sunset, it's close."

For months I followed that path. If I came from East Bay, I'd get off at Embarcadero BART Station and take the MUNI train. If I came from dance class, I'd get off at Civic Center and take the MUNI. I found it was a few cents cheaper than going all the way to Embarcadero before transferring.

After Sunset, there would be an O'Reilly Auto Parts on the right, then a CVS on the left. Across from the CVS was a Chinese market. Sometimes I'd go there to get tofu and mushrooms and broccoli for our dinner, then walk the few blocks to The Pilot's place, past the Thai restaurant.

To go back to Berkeley, I'd wait for the L-Train to pick me up in front of the gardening store that also sold marijuana supplies. The L-Train would take me all the way to Embarcadero, and I'd BART back to Rockridge and take a bus to my apartment.

In-Flight Entertainment

There's a scene in *The Two Towers* where Lord Elrond tells the lovesick Arwen to board the ship to the undying lands of Valinor, for there is no longer hope in Middle-earth. Arwen reassures Elrond, and herself, that there's still hope. But Elrond shows her a grim prophecy, that even if Aragorn is the victor over Sauron and becomes king, even if Arwen gets her wish to marry Aragorn, she will live long after Aragorn's death, for she is half-elven.

"And there will be no comfort for you, no comfort to ease the pain of his passing," Elrond proclaims.

In the book's appendix, "The Tale of Aragorn and Arwen," it was said that Arwen lived until the winter after Aragorn's death, after which she bade farewell to her children and her people and stepped into the forest Lothlórien and laid herself on Cerin Amroth, the heart of the forest, the mound on which she and Aragorn had plighted their troth. And there, on the mound covered by the falling mallorn-leaves, Arwen died.

The Pilot and I were on his bed when we watched this scene. My head was on his chest. He was already asleep. I kissed his forehead goodnight and turned off the television and the lights.

Critical Error

"I'm ugly," I said.

"I'm so tired of you saying that," The Pilot said. "Why don't you open an account on a hook-up app? I'm sure you'll get plenty of men."

"You don't mind?"

"You're young. You need sex. Lots of it. And it's good for your confidence."

"What if it does the exact opposite? What if I don't get anything?"

"Trust me, you will," he said.

I created a profile on a gay dating site. A few months later, The Musician sent me a message.

Force Majeure

"If only you were American," you said. *If only*, I thought, as I sat sideways on your lap on your reclining chair at your house near Ocean Beach, your arms tight around me like a tourniquet.

"DOMA is no longer in effect," I said. "We can be together."

"It's not that simple," you said.

I didn't get it, but I didn't pursue it. Being with you was one of those rare moments when I was able to not think of anything but the present, but your words awakened my dormant worries. Maybe it was for the best. The prospect of spending the rest of my life with someone twenty years older was terrifying. We wouldn't exactly be growing old together.

What would my parents say? Would they stop us the way Elrond stops Aragorn from being with Arwen? After you're gone, will I then realize it is too late to start all over again? Will Jakarta ultimately be my Cerin Amroth? But I'm no elf, and you're not a Dúnedain.

There were too many reasons. The Musician was one of them.

Check the Manual

"The way Asians work," you said, "is that you don't tell someone you don't like him."

"What do you mean?" We were having dinner at a Thai restaurant in downtown San Francisco. It was late September and the city was freezing.

"Someone you don't like sends you a message, then you reply, then that person thinks you like him too, but you're just too nice to say no thank you. And one day you just disappear. No words, no trace. Poof. Gone."

"That's not true," I said. "Not all Asians are like that."

"I hope you aren't like that."

I didn't answer. I was guilty as charged. I did that to The Baker.

Human Error

Why were you so bitter? Why couldn't you stop talking about how religions ruined humanity? Why couldn't you stop complaining about young Asians who wouldn't give you the time of day? Why couldn't you stop saying that one day you'd lose me to a tall, blond man? You'd been saying that even before I'd met The Musician. Were you a psychic?

Why did you have to shout in the theater? I had to cover my face with my hoodie after you shouted, "Just kill him!" when we were watching *Star Trek Into Darkness*. Why did you think it was acceptable to wear a loose pair of jeans and Nike shoes and a black canvas jacket with Batwing sleeves that were tapered around the wrists when we went to see *The Shining* at a very hipster theater? Everyone dressed and looked the same hipster way: boots, leggings or tight jeans, tiny backpack, oversized glasses, graphic t-shirts, and messy hair. Why couldn't you?

But worst of all, why was I not jealous when you said you'd gone to a sex club while I was away in Indonesia that summer to do research on drag queens? Why was I not jealous when I saw you gawk at those practically naked boys at Castro Street Fair? I don't have the answers to why you were bitter. Someone once thought it was a good idea to start analyzing me when I didn't even ask for it. He told me the reason why I didn't want to write sad stories was because I didn't want to feel sad. I felt violated afterward. I should've responded with something like, "The reason why you go to a therapist is because you need someone to tell you what mental issues you're having so that you can just name them and blame them and not yourself for the things you do to people who love you," and then I should've left him, but I didn't, not until he gaslit me and crippled whatever confidence I had. I didn't want to stoop that low and start analyzing you. But I recognized my problems and I knew damn well why I wasn't jealous.

Mayday

The Pilot was waiting for me when I arrived at his house. There was a big box on the table.

"What's this?" I asked.

"Open it," he said.

It was the enameled pewter peacock ring holder. The one I saw in Chinatown. The one I couldn't take my eyes off.

"I couldn't," I said.

"You've given me a lot. And I don't mean the Weyland-Yutani mug and the laptop cooling pad. The past few months I felt like I've found true happiness. Going to the gym feels easier. Flying feels easier. I have a reason to go home."

"It's going to be out of place in my apartment."

"You can just put it here."

So I did.

"Are you going anywhere on Thanksgiving?" I said.

"Yeah. Flying assignment to Chicago. Sorry."

"That's fine."

When The Pilot was sleeping, I made plans with The Musician. I told him that I could come to LA to spend Thanksgiving with him and his friends.

Major Malfunction

A rebound is still a relationship. Like all relationships, it can end badly. The one thing that's noticeable in a rebound is that the presence of the rebound partner is always forced. I turned The Pilot into a Frankenstein monster, I stitched in him the preserved, hand-picked memories of previous partners who had left me. It wasn't long before I realized that The Pilot couldn't be all of those things. He wasn't young. He wasn't tall. When we were waiting for the train and he held me from behind, he couldn't rest his chin on my shoulder and that bothered me. When we were busy working with our computers, me with my writing assignments and him with his flying assignments, I stole a glance at him and there he was, wearing his farsighted glasses, his head jutted out like a turkey's, never close enough to the monitor to read the small font, his lips pursed in deep concentration. He might as well have been sixty years old.

As these truths uncovered themselves, the more time I spent with him, the more I realized that I was still comparing him to other men. That although I'd given up the idea of turning him into my own Frankenstein memory monster, I still couldn't accept his imperfections. He wasn't significant enough to stop the idealized memories of my former lovers. That was when I knew he was only a rebound partner, and would only stay that way forever.

Signal Lost

"Listen," he wrote. "I don't know what's going on. You've been silent the whole time."

"You changed," another text read. "Was it something I did? Was it something I said?"

Another one arrived a day later.

"All right. If you choose to leave, at least return the key. I'll be on a flight assignment, so just drop it through the mail slot."

Last Transmission

It was Wednesday night in early December. Ten p.m., more or less. I was on my way to The Pilot's house after school. It was cold and I was hungry.

I realized it would be the last time I'd take the L-Taraval train to Ocean Beach, past Sunset, past O'Reilly Auto Parts and the Thai restaurant on the right. On the train, I wrote him a vague letter saying there were other elements at work and they didn't allow us to continue our relationship. I couldn't write that I'd found someone who was taller, better dressed, wasn't allergic to cats, and who made me laugh until my sides hurt. My handwriting was terrible and the ride made it even worse.

I stopped by the CVS two blocks away from his house, for an envelope and some Twinkies.

His street was cold and dead. My boots made piercing clacking noises every time they hit the sidewalk. I walked and walked and couldn't find the house in the darkness. I was almost at the end of his block and I turned back. I'd passed it. I didn't know how I'd passed it. I walked back and finally saw The Pilot's old black Ford sedan. It was parked in the driveway.

The door was locked. I thought about the peacock. Should I go in and get it? Will that qualify as breaking and entering? I decided that it would and I slid the envelope down the mail slot. Everything was so quiet that I could hear the envelope land behind the door.

A few months later, I found the Twinkies in my bag, still sealed, but smushed flat.

ODE TO SUNSET STEPS

You hadn't locked the front door of your house.

"It's a safe neighborhood," you always said. It was, but you were too trusting. "You want to see the sunset? I found a nice spot when I went jogging."

"Aren't you tired?" you'd just returned from flying assignments. San Francisco, Los Angeles, Hawaii, New York, San Francisco.

"I took a nap," you said.

"My ankles hurt." I'd tried on a new pair of sandals and wore them during an excursion in Oakland and Berkeley to accompany a friend who was looking for a Halloween costume. He wanted to be Alice of *Alice in Wonderland* and his fiancé would be Dorothy of *The Wizard of Oz*. My ankles were bleeding heavily when I came back to my apartment.

"We can drive," you said.

And we did.

There they were. The Tiled Steps. They were on Sixteenth Ave and Moraga Street. I could remember the place clearly because of the names. I get off at the Sixteenth Street BART Station to get to my dance studio and my school is in Moraga. What were the odds? I could easily remember the date the Steps were officiated. My mother's birthday. She's a Virgo. Just like you. Only two days apart.

"Virgos are always right," you'd said when we had one of our mock-fights. "But if your mother and I met, then I'd be the correct one." There were days when I thought about it and some days I doubted it.

The Steps had seven landings. From below, one could see how carefully they were designed. Swirls of waves and sunrays. They looked like a mosaic out of van Gogh's painting. They reminded me of *Starry Night*. With red round glasses that looked like cherry trees and names of people and families and local businesses.

To our dear mother. The family of Chavez. Al's Electric.

They were written on a cloud or a bird or a fish.

"I'm surprised it's empty," you said. There weren't that many people. A group of four people was on top of the stairs. An older couple was climbing with us. They nodded and smiled at us and we nodded and smiled back, saying our hellos and good-days. You searched for my hand. You found it.

We climbed the five subsections of the Steps. Each time stopping and turning around to look at the orange sun just inches above the horizon. Well, inches from where we were anyway. Isn't perspective amazing?

"Let's sit here," you said. We stopped at the top of the sixth landing.

"Why?" The seventh's gleaming swirls of red and yellow invited me to climb up further. My bleeding ankles were covered with bandages and secured by my socks and boots. They didn't feel painful.

"If you sit on the very top, the tree will block the view."

There was a big tree, its branches and leaves hovering above us, covering the setting sun.

We sat down. I was near the wall and you were on my right. I kissed your left cheek, your eyes hidden by the Oakley sunglasses. Their iridescent lenses a shade of peridot and sapphire blending together. I rested my head on your shoulder.

A black poodle stopped on your right. Its black muzzle moist and nudging your arm. You gave it a pat. Its owner climbed down from behind us and the black poodle followed him.

"That dog is a tease," you said as we saw the dog trotting past strangers, letting them pat its head or back for three seconds and then leaving them wanting more. I kissed your cheek again.

I could see the white and bubbly waves of the ocean in front of us, but I couldn't hear them growl. I couldn't hear them crash. Everything was still. Even the woman who was climbing the stairs and taking photos of the setting sun with her phone. No crickets. No geckos.

"Don't stare at the sun," you said. "You'll go blind."

I'd been staring at it. I could not not stare at it. The way it would drown in mere minutes now. Ten minutes had passed. We had the best seat.

"Too bad there's fog," you said. You explained something about the fog, how it covered the horizon. A white line of low clouds.

"I don't mind."

Everything was awash in amber lights. Like a camera filter.

"There we go," you said. A suspended egg yolk.

The bottom tip of the egg yolk touched the top of the ocean. And then it began to sink. Down, down, down.

"Don't stare at it."

How could you not stare at it? How could the orange glow bleed with the static blueness of the sky and produce bursts of rose pink?

"When was your last sunset?"

"August, in Bali," I said. It was with The Baker, at the

beach near his house. Soft silver sand bore our footsteps, bubbles of waves swirled around our toes and swallowed our ankles and knees and thighs.

The last bit of the sun sank even slower. The embers seemed as though they didn't want to perish, as though they were fighting for air, to breathe above water, until they finally gave up and the sky was a vast sea of indigo.

"I wish I'd brought my big camera," I said.

"We'll return one day," you said. I liked that. "Let's get dinner."

I kissed your lips and we climbed down.

We never got the chance to revisit the Steps.

CRYO

Our memories can be dormant. This happens naturally after the death of a person or an animal, or a destruction of a place, or after not seeing someone or something for a long time. Some of us work hard to preserve our memories, but in doing so, we sometimes inadvertently freeze them. This is why some of us can never look at a swastika. This is why some of us will always think Michael Vick is a monster. This is why some of us yearn to return to that first kiss or that first love. Some of these memories will never get out of the cryo chamber.

This had happened to my mother. My fear of aging and its fatal consequence forced me to subconsciously put my memory of her in stasis. She was always a taller, slender woman in her forties, with gleaming black, shoulder-length hair. This happened for ten years. One day, when we were at a store we'd frequented and my mother was wandering around, the salesgirl asked me if she was my grandmother.

The carefully constructed image of my mother that I had projected through that preserved and frozen memory was annihilated. My mother aged before my eyes. I realized how small she was, a good several inches shorter than I was. Her hair was no longer gleaming, nor was it black. She had wrinkles and aging spots. She no longer wore fitting clothes and that made her look dumpier. Her fleshy arms and hands were handling a grey shoulder bag that another salesgirl had given her to inspect.

"No," I said. "She's my mother."

Looking back, I'm glad that I was asked that question because it jolted my memory of my mother back to life, enabling it to grow with her, pushing the outdated memory of her thin and flat against the walls and into the corners. But I can never forgive myself for allowing ten years to pass without adding a single memory of my time with her.

MOVING DAY

It was the end of May. I just graduated with two MFA degrees and was dreading going out into the real world, worried that those discouraging Yahoo! Career articles had been right all along.

The Musician and I had loaded his station wagon with boxes and boxes of my stuff: books, manuscripts, photography equipment, clothes, accessories, DVDs, and a million tiny things that took up space. Fitting the boxes inside the car was a combination of a jigsaw puzzle and Jenga. It was one of those moments that made me wish I were Buddhist. Or at least not a hoarder.

I waved goodbye to the greenish-beige Samsonite suitcase that my mother had bought me three years earlier. It was already torn in a lot of places although the zippers were still good and wheels were still functional. We left it on the sidewalk, hoping that someone would give it a better home.

Leaving Berkeley was a good decision. Leaving NorCal, in general, was a good decision. I was moving on, away from external factors that would jeopardize my relationship. As we drove out of the parking lot and turned right onto Telegraph to get onto the I-5, I felt ready to start a new life, on a clean slate, but I realized that moving geographically had nothing to do with moving on.

We may try to compartmentalize and isolate each story, like an area on a map that has clear boundaries. In real life, this is harder to do. Stories will blend. Boundaries blur. Although I've crossed into another place, remnants from the previous realm are still stuck to my shoes. Some of them, like dirt and dust, can fall off easily, but blades of dried grass and burrs get in all over. Including hiking boots. The years I lived there, California was so dry that there were dried burrs everywhere. They pierced through the material and stayed there and I wouldn't have a choice but to sit down and pick them out of my shoes before resuming my journey.

And before you suggest plastic rain boots because they're waterproof, dustproof, vegan friendly, and you're sure burrs can't pierce through that kind of material, let me ask you this: would you go hiking wearing rain boots? Would you go across the desert wearing rain boots? Would you go to a formal restaurant wearing rain boots? You can't have the beauty of Christian Louboutin stilettos and expect them to be as comfortable as Crocs. Not everyone has the privilege of owning more than one pair of shoes. We can't all be Imelda Marcos. Even she had to leave some of her favorite pairs behind when she ran away. Some of us can't even afford these metaphorical shoes and have to deal with metaphorical splinters and metaphorical sharp gravels and metaphorical rug burns.

But if we're lucky, we will have someone who stops with us once in a while, someone who helps remove the dust or sand or burrs that are stuck to our shoes or the splinters that get under our skin, someone who helps us mend our shoes, someone who carries us when we can no longer walk, and all our books, manuscripts, photography equipment, clothes, accessories, DVDs, and a million tiny things that take up space. And if we're luckier, we will be that someone.

TIME

It was Thursday night. Barely ten minutes past nine. Ario was sitting in the car in the parking lot of Glendale Galleria with Nina Simone in his ears. He couldn't go home. Not yet. His student had cancelled at the last minute and he'd had two hours to kill. He'd spent more than an hour going up and down Bloomingdale's and Macy's and Target, wandering in and out of stores, touching shoes, pants, shirts, ties. He'd run out of cigarettes and he was too cheap to buy some. Plus smoking meant he'd need to drive somewhere else because he couldn't smoke in the parking lot.

Stupid country with all the stupid rules, he thought.

Six months ago, he'd seen The Sculptor on his knees on the floor of his workshop room, performing fellatio on an Asian. The Asian boy's hair was styled side-part pompadour. The hairstyle that Ario had always wanted, but could never pull off because he had thin, fine hair. Ario hadn't known how to react. He'd always known his husband was having sex with other people. The signs were there: the bottles of lube by the bed had been moved, some old towels were in the washing machine on a non-laundry day. But this was the first time he'd ever witnessed it.

He should've known when he walked into the door and found two glasses of wine. He should've known when he found a pile of clothes in the hallway. Dark brown loafers, Forever21 Men. Grey shorts with micro houndstooth pattern, Banana Republic. White boxers, Fruit of the Loom. All stacked one on top of the other. He'd wanted to take a photo of them. They looked like a well-dressed, albeit prêt-à-porter, gay contemporary version of Aphrodite's shell in Botticelli's painting. But he couldn't stop walking farther and deeper inside the house. The door to the workshop room was wide open. He'd seen everything but he'd slipped away unnoticed. He'd walked out of the house and driven around until he found a quiet spot to think. Should he call his mother? Should he call his friends? But what could they do? He wanted to go home.

Nine-fifteen. Ario groaned. Has it only been five minutes? Ario thought.

How old was that boy? He looked young. At least five years younger. Could be more. Ario couldn't compete with someone that young, or someone who looked that young. Someone with better hair. And presumably American citizenship. Someone who wouldn't give The Sculptor his life in exchange for a green card. Someone equal to The Sculptor.

And being equal means having power, and power is sexy.

Ario knew this would happen. The Sculptor had told him early on in their relationship that he would get bored, that he would start playing around. Ario thought he could handle it, but he didn't know it would be this soon. Ten months after they'd known each other. Four months after they'd been married.

Nine-twenty. Are you kidding me? Ario groaned again.

Ario pulled the lever on the side of the seat so he could recline. Semi-horizontal. He opened his phone to check Facebook. A friend from school just had a baby. He posted the picture of his wife in the hospital bed, the baby in her arms. Like. A girlfriend had a promotion dinner with her friends.

She'd taken Ario's job. He'd recommended her to his boss, and now she was a high-flying lifestyle editor. Had he waited, the job could've been his. Like, nonetheless. His mother just got on Facebook and she posted a puppy video. Like.

What would Mother think about all of this?

Nine-thirty.

On to Instagram. Oh look, his friends from college posted half a dozen photos from their vacation in the Moluccas. Blue sky. White sandy beach. Smoked fish on skewer. What he wouldn't give to be with them. Heart. Heart. Heart. Heart. Heart. Heart.

Nine-thirty-three. Time was starting to fly. Maybe next time he'd drive up to the beach in Santa Monica where Jane takes Blanche in *Whatever Happened to Baby Jane?*

His phone beeped. It was only from eBay. The used Stella McCartney Falabella bag just dropped fifty dollars. It was still eight hundred dollars more than he could afford. His watch list was littered with things he'd wished to get. More art supplies. He needed new brushes. Maybe the ones that came with a bag of their own. And brush cleaners. He also would like to try painting on silk. He needed to go to the fashion district for some silk. Maybe white. Or crimson.

Ario looked up "Baby Jane beach" on his phone. Apparently, Bette Davis said it was actually built on a sound stage because Joan Crawford couldn't take the heat.

Nine-forty-five. A drive to the beach sounds awful anyway, Ario thought.

He imagined The Sculptor had put on his clothes. He imagined the Asian boy had put on his underwear, his shorts, his shirt, his shoes. He imagined The Sculptor had walked the Asian boy to the door and kissed the Asian boy goodnight. Ario felt bile building up in his stomach. He pulled the lever and the seat jerked back up. A galactic silence surrounded him.

Months ago, he would've still been crying whenever his student cancelled and he had to spend time in the parking lot on Thursday nights with the images of the Botticelli pile of clothes asserting themselves over and over again. Now it was just boredom.

Nine-fifty-six. Good enough.

Ario started the car and began his journey to The Sculptor's house.

HOUSEHUSBANDS

"Was it difficult?" I asked. "The interview?"

Ario and I were sitting in a bakery in Highland Park that Thursday. He'd insisted that we did teatime the proper, English way. I had no idea how he could manage staying thin while scarfing down all those scones and putting that much sugar in his tea. Perhaps the cigarettes helped.

"The one who handled us was a tart," he said. "There was something about her that made me feel uncomfortable. The way she looked down on me. Fat cow. She must've thought I couldn't speak English. Then I opened my mouth and began talking with my British accent and it didn't take us more than ten minutes to be approved."

"Is that what they're after? People who don't really speak English?"

"What did your lawyer say?"

"We haven't discussed it. We just did a preliminary meeting. Introduced each other. Gave him our backstory."

"They'll check for inconsistencies. Hopefully you'll get one who won't put you in separate rooms while you're being interrogated. I mean interviewed."

Our lawyer told us that. I didn't think it was going to be too challenging. The Musician and I just needed to get our bases covered.

"Oh, bollocks," Ario said and I heard someone cry his name. It was a high-pitched wail. If it had been higher, only dogs would've been able to register it. I turned around to see the owner of the voice—a young Asian man in his early twenties with gorgeous coffee-brown skin. He was wearing a mustard muscle shirt, very appropriate for the weather, and very appropriate for his muscular arms that were covered in tattoos. He held a gold motorcycle helmet in his hand.

"How have you been? We haven't spoken in ages! You didn't return my emails, my texts, I thought something happened to you," the young Asian bombarded Ario with questions and hugs and kisses. Ario's face was flushed. I realized that everyone was looking at us, especially at this short, prancing muscle pup who'd just zigzagged around the tables and spoke in a foreign language.

"This is Jaya," Ario said. Jaya and I shook hands.

"It's our first time here. We were just in Silver Lake."

"Jaya lives in Malibu," Ario said. "Wait, who's we?"

"Swanky," I said. "I did a shoot once on a beach in Malibu."

"You model?" Jaya asked.

You must be shortsighted, I thought. "No. Photographer."

"I need a photographer," Jaya said.

"Who's we?" Ario asked. "Is your husband here?"

"No. My boyfriend. My husband's on a business trip. Like always."

Wait, what?

"He's a fitness model," Jaya said. "Trying to be an actor. Like everyone else in LA, am I right? So he needs headshots and physique shots and whatnot. You have a business card? Give me. Oh, there he is."

It was afternoon and the sun was low enough to shine through the windows behind him. East Asian. Cropped hair with faux-hawk. Boots, blue jeans, white wife-beater. A gold-tinted helmet in his hand. Shiny aviators covered his eyes. If it were a movie, The Commodores' "Brick House" would be playing when he walked in.

"Mother Teresa. Is he a Calvin Klein underwear model?" Ario said.

More like an Andrew Christian model. Look at that bulge. Mighty, mighty.

"I've always wanted a Korean," Jaya whispered to us, and then he switched to English. "Was parking difficult?" His English had a strong Indonesian accent.

"Not really," The Model said. He was a good foot taller than Jaya. He reached down, slid his arms around Jaya to cup his butt, and kissed his lips.

I turned away. Ario didn't look too overjoyed with the alarming public display of gay affection. "Give him your card," Ario snapped his fingers. "Quickly, please."

I reached into my purse and took out a card. Jaya and The Model were still standing in front of us. Giggling. Forehead to forehead.

Ario cleared his throat. Jaya introduced us to his boyfriend. His handshake grip was electrifying. What a winning hand.

"What would you like, Babe?" The Model asked. Ario rolled his eyes.

"Red velvet cupcakes!" Jaya said, and The Model went to the counter. "Isn't he great?"

"And your husband isn't aware of his existence, I'm guessing?" Ario said in English, loud enough to reach other tables.

Jaya just giggled. "Do you need money?" he called out to The Model.

"Could you not shout in public?" Ario flicked his wrist.

"I got it, Babe," The Model said. I caught him winking at Jaya.

"Dirt poor and still buying me things," Jaya said. "He's just been hired to model this line of shirts. So we're celebrating. But he hasn't been paid yet."

The Model came back with a paper box.

"Okay," Jaya said. "We need to run. I'll be in touch with you for the shoot."

They walked hand in hand out of the bakery, toward the sun. It actually looked as cheesy and as romantic as it sounded. And the crowd sighed.

"That," Ario said, "was Jaya."

"He's married?"

"To an old toad. Extremely rich. I've been to their Malibu home. Beachfront. His bathroom is bigger than our garage."

"And he's okay with that?"

"With the house? Why wouldn't he?"

"No, I mean with the marriage."

Ario shrugged. He held his tea mug tightly with both hands. I could still see the steam swirl up from his drink. "Oh, to be young and beautiful."

"Bitch, please." I stirred my own ginger tea, waiting for it to cool down, wondering why I'd ordered a scorching hot drink on a scorching hot day, wondering how and why some people just had to have everything: a house in Malibu, a hot boyfriend, a hot body. Maybe I should go on a diet. Join a gym. Go to a dentist.

"Finish your cheesecake and let's go," Ario said. "I need to smoke."

"I'm not hungry anymore," I said and pushed my plate away.

Ario groaned. "What a waste." He finished my cheesecake in five gulps.

PERMANENT RESIDENT CASE

FILING CHECKLIST

Foreign Spouse:
- Completed I-485 form

- Four passport-style photos

- Copy of I-94 and visa page from passport

- Copy of birth certificate and translation

- Copy of marriage certificate (and divorce and/or death certificates if married before)

- A personal check (or money order) made out to Department of Homeland Security for $1,490

- Comprehensive medical exam (including HIV test) and all immunizations by USCIS-approved practitioners and completed I-693 form

American Spouse:
- Completed I-485 form

- One passport-style photo

- Copy of US birth certificate or, if born outside of the US, copy of naturalization certificate

- Copy of marriage certificate (and divorce and/or death certificates if married before)

- Job letter from your employer stating amount of salary

- Copy of last three pay stubs

- Copy of last year's federal taxes, including W-2s or 1099s (but excluding California taxes).

- The first 2 pages of the 1040 form if not self-employed

- A copy of the Schedule C form if self-employed

JAYA

Ario and I are lucky in a lot of ways. We were born with silver spoons in our mouths, or, in Ario's case, a complete set of blood-diamond-encrusted platinum tableware, which explains why he has such a big, vile mouth. Our parents are open-minded, and at least one of them had a Western education. We were raised in the best neighborhoods in Jakarta, the city that for decades has been the most modern, in both technology and way of thinking. We both went to fairly progressive Catholic schools. (Although for a while, when I was in junior high, my all-male Jesuit school did try to separate my gay best friend from me, in the hopes of lessening our faggotry. Obviously it didn't work and we both became queens in our own classroom.) Ario and I had our Bachelor's degrees from reputable universities in Indonesia, had relatively sweet jobs in a non-homophobic environment that paid for our lifestyle (Ario worked as a reviewer at a travel magazine while I was a public relations executive at a five-star hotel). After a few years, we both quit our jobs to pursue Master's degrees in fine arts because our parents believed that we should do what makes us the happiest. We had our Master's degrees from American universities, each got married to an American, and became bohemian bums in Los Angeles.

The only difference between Ario and me is that he was also born with beautiful bone structure that contributed to his confidence and sexual maturity. When I first saw Ario,

I knew he didn't have problems getting laid in Indonesia, what with his slightly European features, courtesy of his grandmother. Indonesians love that Caucasian look. I had always been so overly self-conscious of my native Indonesian features that I couldn't have been promiscuous, even if I had wanted to. I consoled myself by thinking that had I been just a little bit sexier, I would've slept around and died of AIDS a long time ago.

But for Jaya, whose name means "glory," the good life began when he moved to the US. His is one of those sorry stories that illustrate Indonesia's problems with queers and their culture. Ario called him Cinderella, but I disagree.

Instead of a cruel stepmother and stepsisters, his actual parents and actual siblings hit and bullied him for being flamboyant, for wearing a rose pink ribbon around his neck, for having limp wrists and pinkies that stayed up, for walking on the balls of his feet, and for crossing his legs when he sat. And it wasn't a lonely mansion that he had to clean and mop and scrub. It was a small house somewhere in Central Java. It wasn't magic or enchanted slippers that got him out. It was hard work, perseverance, and luck. He started from being a dishwasher in a small restaurant, then a waiter, then a housekeeper at a three-star hotel an hour away from his house, then assistant chief housekeeper. He moved to Bali and became a housekeeper again, then assistant housekeeping manager while also getting his Associate's degree in Hospitality, but almost didn't finish, what with Bali being Bali, and the freedom jolted him and confused him into sleeping around, partying at gay clubs, being late to work, failing his exams, and almost getting fired. He barely managed it, and that was when he met his husband.

Instead of a charming, young prince who pursued him

and broke the hearts (and feet) of many suitors, it was an old Jewish man. Richer, shorter, with a nose that jutted out a bit too far. And this old Jewish man happened to be too weak for the Bali heat that day, the first week that Jaya started working at the five-star beach resort as a housekeeper. The sixty-four-year-old American was standing at the bungalow balcony when he was slapped by the heat and passed out. Jaya saw this and used his master key to open the bungalow and carry the old man back inside. He turned the air conditioner on and ran to the bathroom to soak three hand towels in cool water. He unbuttoned the unconscious gentleman's shirt, put one towel around the old man's neck, and the other two between each armpit. Then Jaya called the resort clinic. He waited on the old man, refreshing the towels, bringing him some cold water to drink, until the house doctor came.

They were married two months later, on Valentine's day. It was a huge wedding at the mansion. Jaya was twenty-two years old.

AN INVITATION TO WEST

HOLLYWOOD

"And that, Darling," Ario said as he was finishing his story of Jaya, "is how one banks a rich, old fart." We were in downtown LA's fabric district. Ario needed silk for a painting project he wanted to work on.

"Yeah, but he couldn't have known that the old man was gay," I said. "I think he sincerely wanted to help him because he's a good person. And a good employee."

"Oh, he'd known all along."

"How? Did he tell you that?"

"He has this amazing gaydar. Just amazing. And he's determined to get out of Indonesia. And when DOMA was struck down, he went all out on the hunt. It was all perfect timing. Now he lives in a beach mansion in Malibu, and you don't even want to know how much monthly allowance he gets."

I was curious, but I didn't want to ask. Envy is my greatest sin. "His husband is okay with him dating someone else?"

"Looks like it. Some people have all the luck," Ario said. "Darling, you once told me you felt like Iris Apfel. Well, if that's the case, then I'd be Coco Chanel. Jaya would be Eva Peron."

I exhaled.

"I know, right?" Ario said. "In the end, it was the poor peasant who got married to the powerful man."

After years of abuse and being unloved and told that he couldn't be what he really was, Jaya got what he wanted, and I believe he deserved it.

"Speaking of marriage, congratulations on yours. Sorry I couldn't come."

"Thanks," I said. "And that's all right." Ario probably would've been rolling his eyes so hard the whole night when they weren't glued to his phone.

"How do you feel?"

"Like nothing's changed. Like it was just a night of us getting together with some friends, and it so happens that we also signed a paper saying we're married."

"We had that too. It was small. About fifty people. We had it in the backyard. Some of my friends from the East Bay came. Some of my Indonesian friends from high school also came. They live in LA."

"Were you happy?"

"I was ecstatic. We had flowers and cake and champagne. People toasted us. Some roasted us. We had a slide projector playing and my high school friends showed everyone what I looked like in high school. Those bastards—but it was beautiful. I felt like I'd accomplished something, you know?"

"Like what?" I said.

"Being married. It's a big thing. It's a big commitment. And to have my Indonesian friends come and support us. I didn't know they'd be that open-minded. I went to a Catholic school, remember?"

I also went to a Catholic high school. An all-male one at that. I didn't have that many friends and there were days when I dreaded going to school because some of my classmates were mean. But we were in junior high and they were twelve or thirteen years old and children are cruel. Years later, at a reunion, I met the same people who had bullied me and we didn't even talk about it. It was all water under the bridge. After The Musician and I were married, I told my classmates over WhatsApp school group convo and made sure they knew I got hitched to a man. My phone was flooded with congratulatory notes.

"I love the Fashion District," Ario said. We were walking in a building with vendors selling bootlegged DVDs and video games on plastic bright orange tarps. "I think it's the most third-world place in LA. It makes me think of Jakarta. It makes me homesick. I think it's this crazy and third-world not because of the crazy homeless people, but because this place is run—and overrun—by immigrants. Anyway, Jaya wanted to meet us at The Abbey."

"Not WeHo Abbey?" I asked.

"There's only one The Abbey. Why? What is it?"

Oh, nothing. It's just that it's the gay capital of beauty is all, and The Abbey is the epicenter, and I'll probably be like fish out of water, a mutt in a dog show, a donkey in a horse race. Hee haw. Can't wait.

TROIS GNOSSIENNES

They walked together. Not in a row, but in a line. Their tempered and unbalanced gaits synchronized with one another for a few moments before returning to their own rhythm.

The first one shuffled in front, hurried, although he didn't know the way. His shirt the color of royalty, and his short shorts of mourning. He looked dead ahead, avoiding eye contact at all costs. He wondered why the two others had convinced him to walk with them, to roam the streets of West Hollywood, in broad daylight, where everyone could see the blemishes on the back of his sweaty knees, the telltale signs of eczema, his skin the color of excrement. He started to regret the short shorts, the pair that his husband said was tired. He hoped his sock wouldn't slide down and reveal a long, ugly scar from an accident decades ago. Slow down, he forced himself. He worried about getting too sweaty. But he'd also like to get to the restaurant soon. He'd also like to get it over with. There was no shade to hide under. No hole to crawl into.

The second one was basking in all the attention. A youth in his navy blue tank top speckled with white stars, showing off his tattooed biceps of clouds and waves and fish with gold and amber scales. He was the one who knew the way to the restaurant. His strut was cocky, almost bowlegged. Eyes hidden behind tinted shades (one of the secret keys to successful people watching). Bubble butt and sculpted quads filled the couture-ripped olive-grey denims. It cost an arm and a leg to have these arms and legs. And these pecs and these abs and this ass. Passersby passed by the first one to admire the second one, who relished the attention and unleashed the mighty powers of his smiling dimples.

The third one was fixated on whatever was on his phone, half a cigarette burning on his right hand. Tap, tap, swipe. He didn't look up but he never bumped into anyone, or tripped on a curb, or stepped on one of those designer corgis that were also roaming the sidewalk. A woven trilby, an ecru summer shirt, azure Capri pants. A pair of crimson espadrilles bending and flexing under his feet. He wasn't being antisocial. The Internet was just more interesting to him. Tap, tap, swipe. He was reading the news and people's comments about the Australian drug smugglers' execution in Indonesia. The country was globally condemned, but not by him. He was glad his home country carried on with the death sentence. He missed home. He crossed the street behind the other two, eyes firm on the screen of his phone. Tap, tap, swipe.

THE ABBEY

Sometimes, your brain is like a parent and your body is like a child throwing a tantrum. When the brain tells the body to shut up or to wear a condom or to remember to do the Arabesque *after* the shimmy, the body does the exact opposite. And like the child's tantrum, the timing is never perfect.

We were at The Abbey. Just a half hour past the end of lunchtime, yet the place was still packed. My brain had unsuccessfully ordered my body not to sweat, so my eggplant-colored shirt had embarrassing sweat spots on it. Jaya asked us what we'd like to drink. It was on him, he said.

I told him I didn't really drink. I never cared for beer, mead, cocktails, or wine. One time, on a searing hot day, after an excursion in Atwater Village, my husband said he wished he had a boyfriend to go to bars with. We had just finished walking around under the blazing noon sun and I had a headache from squinting. The rest of the day was ruined. I wanted to ask him, "Does it matter if it's a boy? Can't your bar friend be an octogenarian butch lesbian who swears more than I do?"

"Oh, but you must," Jaya said. "It's one of the good things about living here. No shitty Muslim telling you we can't have alcohol." He ordered an appletini and tequila shots. Ario ordered a raspberry mojito. The waiter, a gorgeous twenty-something with trimmed blond scruff, winked at

Ario. Sweat began to drip down my back. I pressed it against the pleather seat. If I said I'd be fine with water, would I also get a wink?

"I'm fine with water," I said. Our waiter didn't wink. Why would he? "And a plate of hummus," I said. Still no wink. He collected our menus and walked away to pass on our orders to the kitchen and the bar.

"He's vegetarian," Ario said to Jaya.

"My husband and I are vegetarians," I said.

"Wow, you guys must be a perfect couple," Jaya said. Ario rolled his eyes.

"Oh, not really. Our tastes overlap, but he has low opinions on some of the things I really love."

"Like what?" Jaya asked.

"He hates Tori Amos and Tim Burton and *Coraline*." The Musician didn't say anything after we watched *To Wong Foo, Thanks for Everything, Julie Newmar* because he knew how important the movie was to me. "He loves Wes Anderson's films. And I hate them."

"*Grand Budapest Hotel* was fab," Ario made a pinch with his thumb and index finger.

I told them I'd walked out of the theater when the cat was thrown out of the window and the movie showed its bleeding, scattered carcass on the pavement below.

"It's just a movie," Ario said. "Get over yourself."

"Well, you're entitled to your own opinion. He shouldn't have forced you to watch it with him, especially after you've made clear that you didn't want to see it," Jaya said. "Oh my God," he put his hand on his chest.

"What? What?" Ario looked around. "Please tell me Miley Cyrus just walked in."

"I love this song!"

Ario groaned. I didn't know whose song it was.

"It's Lana Del Rey," Jaya said.

"I don't like her," I said.

"I hate her," Ario said. "She glorifies suicides."

"What? How can you guys hate her? She's amazing. She's perfect. You guys are crazy."

Ario kept on saying bad stuff about Lana Del Rey just to get reactions from Jaya. I was tempted to say, "Gee, whatever happened to us being entitled to our own opinion?" but I didn't know Jaya that well. I saw our waiter walk to the table with our drinks and I shut my mouth, afraid to show my teeth. Maybe then he would wink at me?

There were tiny glasses with dark amber liquid, colorful drinks for Ario and Jaya in curved glasses and just a tapered glass for my clear, tap water. My insecurities made me believe that the waiter had put my water down rudely, as though underscoring the fact that I didn't belong at The Abbey. It could be worse, though. We could be next door at Pump where someone would most likely mistake me for a badly dressed-up basset hound. Or a pug. I wondered what their policy on non-service animals was.

"So many Asians," Jaya said after he'd downed his second tequila shot. "This place is going downhill." Ario and I exchanged glances.

"Hey, I resent that. We're Asians too," I said.

"Do you know what Asians are good at?" Jaya said. "Asians are good at destroying the world. I read somewhere that the last male northern white rhino is now protected by guards with rifles because poachers will kill him, rip his horns out, and sell them for Asian medicine, which, by the way, doesn't do shit. But here we are, Asians."

"Your boyfriend is Asian," I said.

"He's practically white," Jaya said. "He has Caucasian sensibilities, but with an Asian face. No one can resist that."

"Hitler was Caucasian," Ario said.

"Oh, my God." Jaya said. "Don't get me started. You know, he was right. Jews are bastards."

"Your husband is a Jew," Ario said.

"Exactly," Jaya said.

"Hitler was also a vegetarian," Ario said.

"What about Fran Drescher?" I said. "What about Streisand?"

"Jewish men. Male Jews are bastards. They only care about money. You know, those genocides, they make sense. Jews are assholes. So are Armenians. Goddamn mobs and drug dealers." Jaya gulped down the last tequila shot.

"Back when I was at school," I said, "I had an Armenian friend. She was a sweetheart. A cancer survivor. Very polite, very mindful."

"One in a million. No. Armenians deserved to be wiped out from the face of the earth."

I didn't say anything. I didn't want to contradict Jaya. I was still trying to get him to book me as the photographer for his boyfriend. So I let Jaya dig his own grave. I let him hang himself with his words.

"Keep your voice down," Ario said.

"Relax. No one knows Indonesian," Jaya flicked his wrist. "No one speaks it here. It's very unpopular. It's a fucking third-world country that the world condemns, that the world bullies. And I'm tired of being an Indonesian."

"Hey, at least we're not Malaysians," I said. "Or Filipinos."

"Damn right," Jaya burped. "My God. I can't believe some people have it worse than we do."

"Well, I for one am happy that we decided to shoot dead most of the Bali Nine. Those Australians can kiss my Indonesian arsehole for all I care," Ario raised his mojito.

"You'd probably enjoy that," Jaya said. Ario flipped him the bird when he wasn't looking.

Our waiter returned with my nine-dollar hummus.

"What is that thing?" Jaya said.

"You never had hummus?" Ario said.

"It looks like baby's barf," Jaya leaned in, "smells like it too," and ordered chicken quesadillas. I felt a sheer satisfaction as Ario face-palmed himself when we heard Jaya pronounced it "kwe-suh-dilas."

GENTLEMEN PREFER ASIANS

When he wasn't glued to his phone, Ario was always browsing, looking around, watching people. He was an unabashed voyeur and had developed acute peripheral vision as well as mastered the art of discreet eavesdropping. He could silence all the noises around him to tune into a conversation from a table next to us. Jaya was daintily munching on chicken quesadillas, his tattooed bulging biceps betrayed his princess-on-the-dining-table manners, when Ario said, "That's the third one."

"Third one what?" I said.

"Asian boy with an older Caucasian man."

"I wonder why?" I scooped some hummus with a carrot and bit into it.

"Simple. The boy is an immigrant. By the looks of him, Southeast Asian. He doesn't know any better. He just wants to get the hell out of his country although it means being seen out and about as a trophy boy for a troglodyte, which, by the way, is the Latin name of the common chimpanzee."

Two men walked into The Abbey. A Chinese twenty-something and a thirty-something overweight white man.

"What about that guy? He's not old," I said.

"Oh come on. Is that a trick question? Either that's a trick question or you're really clueless," Ario waved at the scruffy blond waiter and signaled that he wanted another raspberry mojito. The waiter gave him a big toothy grin.

"So?" I said.

"He looks like Jabba the Hut. Or should I say, Jabba the Gut. Or Chubba the Gut. Yeah, that's better." Ario laughed at his own joke. "He's a fattie. Flawed. No Asian-Americans will want to fuck that. But beggars can't be choosers. Like Anna Nicole Smith."

"Anna Nicole Smith was white," Jaya said while typing on his phone.

"White trash. Same level as immigrants. And like her, immigrants need ugly, fat Americans, more so than ugly, fat Americans need them."

"Was that why you got married?" Jaya said, still typing.

"That's why all three of us got married," Ario said.

"Your husband isn't an ugly, fat American," I said.

"I lucked out on the looks department, I guess, but sadly not on the patience department."

"I think at least one of us here got hitched for actual love," Jaya glanced at me.

"Really?" Ario turned his head to me. "Would you still marry your husband if you were American?"

The carrot made a satisfying crunchy sound as I chewed and squished it in my mouth. I didn't know the answer. Marrying my husband came with all the risks. I couldn't pick and choose the things I wanted and didn't want. And the whole package included leaving the people I love behind, leaving the country I love behind, leaving a life I'd known for so long behind, starting anew. A somewhat cleaner slate. Ripe with possibilities. And whenever there's possibility, uncertainty hovers close by.

My tongue nudged the carrot-hummus pulp into my throat. I swallowed hard.

"Um . . ."

"See? I told you," Ario looked back at Jaya after I uttered the monosyllabic filler. There was victory in his voice, but he wasn't smiling. "We are exotic creatures. I don't mind being fetishized if I'm given fair compensation. And on top of that, since we need these Americans, we'll take whatever they throw at us. Bones and crumbs, and we'll wag our tails and say, 'Thank you, Master. How very generous of you, Master. I will love you forever, Master,' which is expected of us, since they think we owe them for liberating us from a homophobic country.

"That's why men love dogs. They want a man's best friend to be stupid and dependent and tamable. They want something that's incredibly forgetful and forgiving. Something that will run to them when they call its name. Something they can train to sit, roll over, and play dead. And that, my darling, is why we don't like cats," Ario put his hand on my shoulder.

"That's internalized racism," I said. "You're saying we're so desperate, we so can't do better, that we'll take whatever kind of white man comes our way."

"Your words, not mine."

"I'm not racist," Jaya said. "I love cocks of all races. Especially Asians."

"For once, I agree with you," Ario said. "You're such a whore. A dumb, lucky whore."

Jaya and Ario raised their drinks.

Rihanna was on the speakers. I kept busy with the last carrot nub while Jaya picked on his kwe-suh-dilas. The blond scruffy waiter came over and handed Ario his drink. He smiled as his palm brushed against Ario's hand, but Ario couldn't be bothered. Not even to say thank you.

The loud beep from Jaya's phone gave me a chance to

check mine. No messages. No Facebook likes. No retweets. Not even an eBay alert.

"I've to go. My boyfriend's done with his shoot," Jaya waved at the waiter, asking for the check.

"Me too," I said. "Date night."

The waiter came with the bill. I put cash on the table.

Ario looked at everyone and finished his new drink. He fumbled with his wallet.

"I got this," Jaya said. He put his credit card on the tray and took my money.

HE WHO MUST NOT BE NAMED

Ario didn't even stumble. He'd downed a second glass of mojito and he didn't even stumble. He walked on a straight line. He was about to whip out his phone from his pocket when he grabbed my wrist and cursed.

"What?" I asked.

"That's my ex," Ario said. Jaya asked which one. Ario pointed at a tall, thirty-something scruffy brunet with a gang of friends standing across the street.

"Oh, hot," Jaya said. Ario told him to shut up.

"One of your Voldemorts?" I asked.

"No, that's *the* Voldemort."

Voldemort saw Ario and smiled and waved. The walk sign turned green and he crossed the street toward us. Ario cursed again. And again.

"Backstory in five seconds," Jaya said.

"He dumped me. Said I was too complicated for him. He now lives in San Jose."

"Sorry."

"He moved on a week after we broke up. That's his boyfriend." He looked like a manlier version of Moby.

"Oh, hot," Jaya said. I elbowed him in the ribs. Hard. Then I apologized profusely because I was worried he would tell me to forget about the photography job.

"Facebook said they've been dating for almost two years now."

"You're still friends with your ex on Facebook?" Jaya rubbed his ribs.

"No. I stalked him. That's how I knew he'd moved on. Oh, bugger, here we go."

"Hey," Voldemort said. "How've you been? You never returned my texts. I thought you were dead. Or worse, got back to Indonesia."

"No. Still alive." I saw Ario clench his fists. "I'm good. You? And how is going back to Indonesia worse than being here?"

"You're such a riot. I'm good. Never better, actually. Just got promoted. We're here to celebrate." Voldemort put his arm around Macho Moby and they kissed. Ario looked away.

"There's my boyfriend," Jaya whispered in my ear. "Introduce yourself. Stall them. I've an idea." He ran off to get to The Model. His height and tinted aviators made him easy to spot.

I stepped forward, but I hesitated. How exactly will I be helping? If any, I'll be a step down. I'll give off the vibe that Ario's desperate now and running with the ugly crowd. But something primordial stirred inside me—an instinct to defend my own kind, no matter how vile my own kind was.

"Hi there!" I stretched the two syllables thin and introduced myself. "You live in San Jose? You're so lucky." I was suddenly acutely aware of my voice. It sounded nasally and insincere. Very Kardashian.

"Why?" Voldemort asked.

"Your downtown is so clean and tidy. I wish I were living there instead of LA. Can't believe you're here for vacation. Although Seattle is nice too. And so is Sacramento, I guess, with the public transportation and all." Finally. A perfect time for verbal diarrhea. Valley-girl style.

"Oh, I know. It's not cheap, though," Macho Moby linked his arms around Voldemort's waist like an oversized bald sling bag.

"We just moved in together," Voldemort said. They kissed again.

"Congratulations," I said.

"Yes. Congrats," Ario said. His toothy smile a closed zipper.

"So, how's life?"

"You already asked me that." Ario shifted his weight from one foot to the other and brought his arms akimbo.

Voldemort laughed. "You're such a riot. How're the paintings?"

Before Ario could answer, Jaya's boyfriend The Model jumped beside Ario and gave him a long and sloppy French kiss that lasted seven Mississippis.

"Look at you!" The Model said. "I was gone for only a few hours and you already got sexier." He pinched Ario's ass and Ario slapped his hand away.

"Uh," Ario said. "This is . . ."

"His fiancé," The Model said and extended his muscular arm to shake Voldemort's hand. Even Macho Moby couldn't stop staring at the Korean god. Jaya was standing on the curb a few yards away. He was smiling, his arms were behind his back, his upper body swayed left and right. He looked like a Japanese schoolgirl bursting with secrets.

I saw Ario's fists unclench. The Model put his arms around Ario, hugging him from behind. "You ready, babe?"

Ario nodded. "Y . . . Yeah. We gotta go. It's nice to meet you again and I wish the two of you all the luck in the world."

Of course he didn't mean it.

"Oh. My. God," Jaya giggled when we were out of sight.

"I've always wanted to do that. Adrenaline!" He was fanning himself with his hands.

"What the fuck was that?" Ario pushed The Model away and snapped at Jaya.

"We were helping you!" Jaya said, still giggling.

"I didn't need help. I was perfectly capable of defending myself, thank you very much. And as for you," he looked at The Model, "how fucking dare you?"

"Hey!" Jaya said, "You don't talk to my boyfriend like that!"

"'My boyfriend,'" Ario made air quotes. "I have one thing to say to you, darling: you are married, which means, you are owned by a man, and it's not this man," Ario said, pointing at The Model. "It's that man who saved you from your village, who took you into his mansion in Malibu, who bought you your Proenza Schouler bag and your Bottega loafers and your Chanel shades to cover the actual, poor, peasant soul that lives under that ugly, black skin of yours. So shut the fuck up."

The Model walked in front of Jaya and Ario, shielding his boyfriend.

"Okay, that's enough. They were just trying to help you," I said, but Ario and The Model were already in a staring contest.

"Babe, please," Jaya said.

"You can say whatever the fuck you want to me, bitch, but if you insult my boyfriend again, I will rip you a new one," The Model said.

"You touch me and I'll make sure my lawyers squeeze every cent out of you. I don't expect there will be much of it, but I'll sure enjoy it," Ario said. He was really asking for it.

Jaya pleaded again and I began to sweat again. But it

was a cold sweat. A few people were openly gawking at us, at these fighting Asians.

"Don't just stand there," Jaya said to me, but I didn't know what to do.

"I don't need this," I said to Ario. "I'm leaving. You can walk home."

But I didn't move. No one moved. More people stopped to stare. The commotion attracted valet staff from a restaurant nearby.

"Guys, please," I said. "Not here. Please."

The Model turned around and walked away. Jaya and I waited a few seconds and we breathed a sigh of relief when Ario calmed his stance. The crowd around us began to disperse.

"I'll text you about the shoot," Jaya said. I nodded and walked to my car. Ario trailed behind me.

ENVY

"That was scary," I said.

Ario adjusted his seat belt. "Really? I thought it would be quite funny if he did punch me."

"Are you crazy?"

"He'd be jailed and Jaya would go back to his husband, and I'd be the hero. Win-win."

"What the fuck is wrong with you? You had absolutely no right to do that to Jaya. He just wanted to help."

Ario scoffed and looked away. Two men and a little girl walked to a car. She giggled as one of the men picked her up and gave her kisses. Ario reached into his pocket and took out a pack of cigarettes. I grabbed it from him.

"Give it back," he said.

"We're not leaving if you're going to be a dick."

"You love dicks."

"Oh, grow up," I said.

"Come on." He kicked the glove compartment.

"Get the fuck out of my car if you're going to be like that," I said.

"This is not your car. This is your husband's car. His name is on the license plate. You have nothing here."

"Okay, that's it. Get out."

But Ario went silent and stayed put. He looked out the window again. The family drove away in a black hatchback sedan.

"I want to be him," Ario said.

"Who? What are you talking about?"

"Jaya. I want his life."

"No, you don't," I said.

"No, I do. I really do."

"Are you hearing yourself? It's Jaya you're talking about. That boy agrees with Hitler. That boy loves Eminem. That's like being gay and a Republican. That's like being a woman and an NFL fan. You don't know what you're saying."

"Do I? Do I really?"

"He's young," I said. "He could be hiding something. No one is that happy, or lucky. I mean, just think about it. He's blowing a sixty-five-year-old dick. I had sex with a sexagenarian once. Or attempted to have sex anyway. It was so hard for him to get it up, and every time he did, he needed to go to the bathroom."

"They don't have sex. Not anymore."

"How do you know?"

"He told me. That poor sod isn't around too often anyway."

"And you trust him? Maybe whenever he comes home to his big mansion, he counts the days, you know? He counts the days to that three-year mark when he can finally take the citizen's test, be an American like he's been dreaming of, and divorce the husband, but we don't know that. Maybe he's worried every day because his husband is so rich and can have anyone he wants and he knows that and he lives in fear because he is easily replaced. Do you want to live like that? Do you want to live in fear?"

"Don't talk to me about living in fear. And anyway, he can't be replaced. He saved his life," Ario said. "At least that old cock has him in his will. At least he'll be compensated for all his troubles. And stop making a big fuss about that charade being his idea. He wasn't even the least bit jealous."

"That's because he trusts you, and his boyfriend."

"Oh, he trusts his moocher boyfriend all right. He trusts that his boyfriend will never be attracted to someone like me. That his boyfriend will still worship him. And the worst thing of all," Ario exhaled, "is that he's such a good kisser."

Ario's shoulders shook and I thought he was trying to be funny, but my giggling stopped when I realized he was actually crying.

"I deserve a good kisser," he said. "I deserve to be desired. Whenever I read news about rape, all I can think of is how lucky those slags were. They had someone who wanted them, who thought they were attractive."

"That's such a sick thought. That's not how rape works."

"How would you know? Have you ever been raped?"

I shook my head.

"That's because you're not attractive."

What? For Ario's sake, I hoped he was actually drunk. I actually wished I'd been drunk too so I could just think it was all a dream. "No. That's because I avoid sketchy places and sketchy people."

"You know the feeling, right? When you perform? All eyes are on you? I get that when I'm teaching French and those kids look up to me and for a moment, I'm their world. Nothing I say is wrong or challengeable."

Ario was right. Being wanted, being needed are perhaps the greatest feelings in the world, because they mean I'm significant, worthy of other people's time and attention.

"It's been five months and seventeen days since my husband and I last had sex," Ario said. "I can't even remember the last time he kissed me."

There was something cold and clinical in his voice and tone. He was just stating bare facts, like an air crash investigation official telling bleary-eyed families who were huddled en masse that there were no survivors. It made me think of my own marriage, if The Musician and I would become like them. Two people living in the same house. Bored with each other. It's the first stage toward a relationship apocalypse. Boredom, followed by annoyance, dislike, and finally hatred. Some people were lucky. They got out of the relationship before the third or fourth stage, thus being able to remain somewhat friends. But how soon would boredom morph into hatred? And boredom seemed to be inherent in the era of hashtags and trending topics, especially with gay couples.

That moment, I finally understood what The Baker had meant when he told me I mustn't be perpetually searching for the better one because now I felt what he'd felt. I feared what he'd feared—the dread that crept into him whenever I appeared bored with him. Soon after boredom, I became annoyed by what he did and what he was and ended up hating everything about him. He was replaceable, I'd thought when I ended our relationship, but I was too self-absorbed to realize that I was just as replaceable.

Ario was crying softly in the passenger seat. I put the cigarette pack back in his hand.

We are all replaceable.

"You just met the reason why I want to be a citizen," Ario lit a cigarette.

"Voldemort?"

"I want to show him that I too can be what he is, have the things he has. The freedom, the power, the life. The ability to go anywhere without a bloody visa."

"Really? That's what you're after? To go anywhere without a visa?"

"Sure. Do you know what that means?"

I shook my head.

"It means the world trusts you. It means the world doesn't think that you're poor, that you're a terrorist."

But the US is poor, I thought. And the US also has terrorists and religious extremists and white supremacists. And there are homophobic states like Louisiana and Texas and South Carolina. Every day I heard stories about queer people, especially youths, being thrown out of their houses. By their own flesh and blood. I heard stories of trans people being assaulted and raped and murdered. Gay children killed themselves after being bullied and no one helped. I moved to a country with police brutality, racism, and virtually no gun control.

Sirens wailed outside the West Hollywood Library parking lot. I tapped Ario's address into my phone map.

And Los Angeles isn't all it's cracked up to be. La La Land is not all gold and glitter. Hollywood is full of liars and dying dreams. Downtown is dirty and run by drug dealers. Malibu is snobbish and lonely. West Hollywood is sad and superficial. Gang violence happens two minutes from where I live.

"Is it worth it?" I asked. Ario blew the cigarette smoke out of the window and I worried that he shouldn't be smoking inside the parking structure.

"I want to go home," he said after several puffs.

I started the car and drove the spiral down and out the building and my phone told me to turn left onto Melrose.

GENTLEMEN SUITE: THE NURSE

He Wasn't Supposed to Live

Not after shrapnel was lodged in his skull. Not after six months of induced coma. Not after serving his time as a private in Iraq.

And yet there he was, making the first move on Ario on a dating site. And yet there he was, texting Ario, promising him that he'd text Ario constantly, when he woke up, before he went to bed. And yet there he was, buying Ario dinner, buying them movie tickets. Kissing him, fondling him, in Yerba Buena Garden, in an auditorium at AMC Metreon, on BART. Two months before Ario left Berkeley to be with The Sculptor, the man he would marry.

They had sex in Ario's apartment.

He was poised to take Ario's heart away from The Sculptor.

He was The Nurse. Ario had wanted to call him The Soldier, but that wasn't what he did. Not anymore.

"My hero," Ario texted him as The Nurse said goodbye because duty called, but he promised he'd text Ario back as soon as he got off work.

So young, so different, so passionate, and perhaps so much more abusive than The Sculptor once Ario got to know him. Maybe instead of a mallet, it would be a baseball bat or a frying pan or a spade. But it never happened.

"I think I'm in love with you," Ario said, as they made

love that Saturday, their second meeting after that disastrous *Pacific Rim* movie.

The Nurse didn't answer. Why should he? He had other friends. He had other playmates. He had other dreams: to get rich, to live in San Francisco's SoMa.

What am I thinking? Ario thought. What am I expecting? You asked me if I had other lovers, I said I did. I asked you if you had other lovers, you said you did.

Core

"Have you told anyone about me yet?" The Nurse texted Ario. He just came back from their date.

"Not yet," Ario replied.

"Oh good! I told my best friend about you but left it very vague."

"Like how vague?"

"I told him that I'm seeing a guy I like and am interested to see where it goes," The Nurse wrote.

"That sounds fair," Ario replied.

Actually no, Ario thought. That doesn't sound fair. Why aren't you in love with me as much as I'm in love with you? Why aren't you smitten by me as much as I'm smitten by you?

"Yeah, I'm working tomorrow morning at 5. Ugh, I have to be up at 4," The Nurse wrote.

"Well, go to sleep. You did a lot today. You were a friend, a godfather, a cook, and a lover."

"Yeah I did! The best part was . . . time with you."

Ario wanted to cut open his chest and put his phone next to his heart.

Flaws

The Nurse misspelled a lot. Instead of "too" he wrote "to." Instead of "condescending" he wrote "condensating."

It's not even a word, Ario thought.

The Nurse downed two, three cups of coffee every day, plus Red Bull. The Nurse loved to get drunk and black out. He was so young.

The Nurse was allergic to dogs. Ario loved dogs and wanted to have several.

The Nurse talked too much about moving to San Francisco from Richmond, making so much money, interviewing at different places to make so much more money. Ten thousand dollars more a year. Money, money, money.

Pillow Talk

"If you were a fuck buddy, I'd fuck you so hard and you wouldn't be able to sit for two weeks," The Nurse said.

"I'm not just a fuck buddy?" Ario said.

"No. I don't treat fuck buddies to dinners and movies."

"Why am I not just a fuck buddy?"

"I don't know. You make me feel special."

"What about that guy in Sacramento?" Ario said

"He's younger. I don't like younger guys."

"How old is he?"

"He's four months younger than I am," The Nurse said.

"That's technically the same age as you," Ario said.

The Nurse chuckled. He tapped Ario's nose with the tip of his finger. Ario flinched on purpose. Cutely.

I'm thirty, Ario thought. You're twenty-seven. You're a baby.

"Younger guys can be so clueless," The Nurse said. "I like older guys. They're more stable. More mature. Wiser.

One time, that Sacramento guy and I were having sex, and he called me a bear. I got so angry."

"Why?"

"I'm not a bear. Bears are big and fat and hairy."

Is that why you go to the gym a lot? So you don't get big and fat?

"Okay. You're an otter then."

"You make me feel special," The Nurse said.

"How so?" Ario said.

"I don't know. You just do."

I'm not sure about those things, Ario thought. I don't have a job, so I guess that makes me less stable.

The Nurse put his head on Ario's chest. His soft, buzz-cut hair tickled Ario's chin. Ario kissed his forehead, stroked his head, trying to remember where the shrapnel wound was, trying not to touch it.

Ario traced the letters of his name on his left shoulder blade. The one covered with a bald eagle tattoo. What are you doing to me? Ario thought.

"Is that a spell? Are you enchanting me?" The Nurse said.

"That's beyond my power," Ario said.

Lore

"Do you want to be in a book?" Ario asked. It was more of a whisper, though. He was half-hoping The Nurse wouldn't hear.

"No," The Nurse said. "I want to be in a lore, you know? Like, 'I know a guy who knows a guy who knows a guy who knows a guy,' and that guy is me."

You deserve more than just some few fleeting passages, Ario thought. Probably not a book, but still. Maybe a painting.

"Is that odd?" The Nurse asked.

"No," Ario said.

Still, I'll acknowledge you, Ario thought. If not in a book, then in my life. I'll give credit to you, for being my saving grace, for listening to me, for being my support system, for sending me text messages of nothings, text messages that I crave so much but won't receive from the man I'm marrying.

End of the Line

Ario texted him from The Sculptor's house. The Nurse had taken the week off for job interviews and to be with his other playmate who lived in Sacramento.

"I'm jealous," Ario wrote.

"Lol why are you jealous?" The Nurse replied.

"I don't know. I get jealous a lot sometimes. But I don't really do anything about it."

Maybe I'm in love with The Nurse because he's young and beautiful, Ario thought. Maybe this one will be short-lived. Maybe I should say goodbye before I get crazy. Crazier.

Ario waited all night for The Nurse to reply.

Rehab

The Nurse and Ario were so disappointed when they walked out of the theater after the movie ended.

"We really should watch something good," Ario said. "It's starting to turn into a habit. This is like, what? Our second date?"

"No, it's our third," The Nurse said.

"I'm not sure the second time we met counts as a 'date.'" He'd come over to Ario's apartment for their second meeting and they had sex.

"Well, we had fun, didn't we?" The Nurse pinched Ario's

ass as they walked out of AMC Metreon. He'd been shoving his tongue down Ario's throat in the auditorium and playing with Ario's nipples and hard penis through his shirt and pants.

Unfortunately that evening, The Nurse couldn't come over. He had to go to his friends' bachelor party. His friends were getting married after being together for seven years.

"I'm worried my ex will be there," The Nurse said.

"Oh, it's the same circle of friends?" Ario asked. The Nurse nodded. "Were they your friends who became his friends or his friends who became yours?"

"We met them at a bar when we were together. So, at the same time, I guess. I'm just hoping that he'll be too busy doing meth to go to the party."

"You mean like crystal meth?" Ario asked.

"Yeah. That's why I left him."

The Nurse had paid for his ex to go to rehab. Twice. He stayed clean for about three months and then went back to doing it.

The Nurse kissed Ario goodbye at the Powell Street BART Station. "Text me when you're home," he said. He stayed by the gate until Ario disappeared underground.

Perhaps I could be so lucky, Ario thought. Perhaps in another lifetime. Perhaps I'm just paying off all my bad karma, all my bad juju, all my bad energies.

He still hadn't told The Nurse that he'd be moving out of Berkeley in three weeks, away from him, to be with the man who threw a mallet at him.

The Nurse Just Got a New Job in Sacramento
"I'll be making $33.70 per hour," The Nurse said. "That means I'll get about $150,000 per year!" He was twenty-seven years old. Rent in Sacramento was only $700 or something.

Ario was with him when The Nurse received the phone call in his beaten-down 2007 Toyota Camry with no power windows and chipped paint. Ario was with him when The Nurse called his sister. His parents. Ario was with him when he texted his instructors. His fuck buddy down in Sacramento with whom he stayed for the interview there. Ario was with him when he nibbled on grilled cheese sandwiches at a diner. The Nurse was too high on adrenaline and Ario was too low on his own stupid emotions.

"Weeks of job interviews, finally some happy news," The Nurse said. "No more wiping people's butts."

"What did your friend in Sacramento say?" Ario asked.

"'Congratulations, you deserve it.'" The Nurse put his phone down a little too roughly after reading the text message. "I was top of my class: 99% in skill evaluation, 92% theory."

"Wow," Ario said. "That's . . . You're a real catch."

"Thanks. What made you say that, though?"

"Well, I don't really care about the money, but you're top of your class, and you have this single-mindedness, this determination to succeed, to get what you want."

"I think you are too," The Nurse said.

"You don't know that."

"What made you say that?"

"I want to leave my mark, you know?" Ario said "I want to do something big. Something meaningful." Ario nibbled on a stale potato chip. "Maybe piss on someone."

The Nurse laughed. "You're so funny."

That's what I do best, Ario thought. I make people laugh. I make myself laugh so I won't know that I'm sad, so others won't know that I'm sad. I'm funny.

"Or a tree," The Nurse said.

"Or a tree. Or a fire hydrant," Ario said.

They walked back to The Nurse's car. He held Ario's hand. They kissed. The Nurse opened the car door. Ario wanted to die.

"You're holding back," The Nurse said as he drove Ario back to his apartment.

"I'm not," he said. "This is how I react to happiness. This is me being happy."

"Wow. You're not used to happiness, are you?"

No.

He parked in the shade in front of Ario's apartment building. They kissed. They kissed. They kissed.

"I want to take you to Sacramento," he said.

Ario wanted to say, I'd like that more than anything. Yes, please take me. Yes, I'd run away with you. But you don't know me. You don't even know why I'm here, why I'm holding on here, in this damn country, thousands of miles away from my home, from my parents, from my friends, from the beautiful life that I used to know.

"I'm so happy for you," Ario cradled his bald head in his arms and kissed his forehead, his right cheek, his right ear.

"I'm so happy for me too," he said.

Ario pushed him away and opened the door.

"Say it," he said.

"Say what?" Ario asked. The Nurse kissed him. He kissed The Nurse back. Three times, four times, five times. "Say what?" Ario asked. Six times, seven, eight. "Say what?"

Ario pushed him away again and got out of the door.

"You're running away?"

"That's what I do best," Ario said. "Drive safely. Go celebrate."

"I will," The Nurse said.

Luck

It was Friday the thirteenth.

"I'm sorry if I didn't look happy. I was and am extremely happy for you," Ario sent him a text message after he got out of The Nurse's car.

"That's okay. What was bothering you?" The Nurse replied.

Ario told him about The Sculptor. Ario told him about the proposal. Ario told him it was the only way for him to stay in the US.

Ario's phone blinked. It was The Nurse. He called. He had to call.

"Do you love him?" The Nurse asked. "You can't go back to Indonesia. It's dangerous there."

Ario was offended. Is that all Americans think of Indonesia? That it's some backward country with Muslim terrorists and homophobes?

"I don't know," Ario said. "I used to really love him, but some things happened along the way, like in most relationships. And now I don't know."

"If I were you, I'd bite the bullet," Ario said. "Do you picture yourself living with him for a long time?"

"How long is long? Four years?"

"Five years. Ten years. You need to stay at least five years to get a citizenship."

Ario decided to bite the bullet.

No More

It had been a day. Almost a day.

The last text message The Nurse sent was the night before. Ario was trying to paint, but it didn't work. It was botched. The Nurse said he finally just got home and was so tired. Ario replied an hour later, saying hopefully he'd gone to bed, sleep well.

It had been twenty-three hours ago, but Ario didn't know for sure because he'd deleted the text messages. He'd deleted The Nurse's number from his phone book. Now he was thinking of deleting The Nurse from his Facebook.

Ario was drunk on champagne from the party thrown for the alumnae of the MA program. He walked back from the bus stop to his apartment because there was no bus. He laughed. He cried. He thought about The Nurse and The Sculptor. He checked his phone for any message from The Nurse and of course there was none and while he was doing that, his face was slapped by leaves on really low branches. It was dark. He laughed. He was drunk. He lit a cigarette. He cried. He laughed again. He sang Streisand's "Funny Girl" in the hallway of his apartment building as he was fumbling with his key until his neighbor told him to shut it.

Ario closed the door behind him and for the first time in a long time, he turned off his cellphone. He couldn't wait to leave Berkeley.

THE DEMONS OF INDONESIA #4:

THE CHRISTIANS

What most people don't know is that homophobia in Indonesia doesn't only belong to Islam.

To be an employee of Sekolah Pelita Harapan, a Christian-based educational establishment that is part of the Christian-based Lippo Group, one needs to agree to a set of values. These values include: ". . . being just in all our dealings with other people; not discriminating unfairly against others because of their race, beliefs, gender, disability, or values;" (Note that they leave out "sexual orientation") and ". . . ensuring that sexual relationships occur only within a monogamous marriage, therefore abstaining from pre-marital [sic] sex, extra-marital [sic] sex, and homosexual activities."

This homophobia is also in the statement of faith of Universitas Pelita Harapan, the Lippo Group university that offers undergraduate and graduate programs. This statement of faith must be signed by all employees.

Under the "Gender Issues" section of the booklet are several points that include (bold print theirs): "Humans as male and female were created by God in the image of God, **equal in dignity**, value, essence and human nature, but with **distinctions in role and function**, especially in the family;" and "We thus **abhor** the all too common **abuse of women** as if they were inferior to men and also **deny** the inappropriate

blurring of distinctions between men and women, especially in their respective roles in the family."

And then: "We believe and affirm that **marriage** is ordained by God as a covenant and intended to be a **life-long** union and relationship between **one man and one woman**;" and "We affirm that any sexual activity should only occur in the covenant relationship of marriage and that any sexual activity outside the covenant of marriage is condemned by God, including same gender sexual relationships. We do not believe that same gender marriage is a legitimate covenant relationship. **God condemns as sinful the practice of homosexuality** as well as the practice of adultery and fornication and other sexual sins, all of which may be forgiven in Christ where there is genuine repentance and faith."

No, I don't know what they mean by "same gender sexual relationships," but they do sound like redneck white trash looking up words in the thesaurus. And one can argue that by writing "same gender marriage," they are actually not against same sex marriage, as long as the two people are not of the same gender. Or maybe whoever wrote the guideline is too ignorant to understand the difference between sex and gender.

The section ends with a note advising the reader to refer to "the 'Danvers Statement' published in 1987 for a faithful and helpful Biblical statement on gender roles and relationships."

Both Sekolah Pelita Harapan and Universitas Pelita Harapan are supposedly modern schools taught mainly in English by Indonesian and foreign teachers. Their subjects include science and the arts. Tuition fees range from USD 5,000 to USD 20,000 per year, not including an annual development fee from USD 2,000 to USD 5,000 (2015).

When Lady Gaga's sold-out concert in 2012 was cancelled due to anarchic pressures by Front Pembela Islam (Islamic Defenders Front, the rogue Indonesian Muslim terrorist group), *The Jakarta Globe*, the local English newspaper that belongs to Lippo Group, ran an editorial entitled "Gaga Concert is Too Hot For [sic] Indonesia." This piece allegedly bypassed the actual editorial team, meaning a higher power sneaked it into the edition. The author wrote that it was "unfortunate that the concert was called off due to security concerns" and reminded the reader that "Indonesia is a vibrant, diverse democracy and as such the authorities had to take into consideration all voices. It is their job to ensure that all segments of society have their voices heard." Then the editorial criticized the messages of Lady Gaga's songs, writing, "There are, however, many justifiable reasons for opposing acts like Lady Gaga, such as the messages these supposed artists project. It is not about how she dresses, which is needlessly provocative, but about what she sings and the lyrics of her songs. It is about the lack of morality in what she represents."

These people and organizations are a menace to those who long for tolerance in Indonesia. They're more dangerous than Front Pembela Islam because Sekolah Pelita Harapan and Universitas Pelita Harapan are supposedly progressive schools and *The Jakarta Globe* is supposedly a progressive news outlet and yet they still harbor latent hatred, disgust, and fear.

CLOSURE

Ario was with The Sculptor when The Nurse sent him a text. They were on their way to Los Angeles. The Sculptor's car was full of Ario's things.

"After a long stretch of silence?" I asked. "What did he say?"

"After two weeks. He asked me how I'd been. I said I was fine. He said he'd blacked out during the Pride Parade. Then he did the strangest thing."

"What?"

"He told me that ever since I left, he'd been with that guy in Sacramento every day. They'd gone exclusive. Then he sent me a photo of them."

"Yeah. That's weird."

"Like, what does that even mean?" Ario asked.

"Can't you guess? He was trying to rub it in. He knew you weren't happy with your husband, so he wanted to show off."

"I wish I'd known him longer. I could've found out that he wasn't all that."

"That text proves that he wasn't all that," I said.

"I thought so too. But I just needed to hear it from someone else. Thank you."

I didn't know what to say. It was the first time Ario had thanked me. In the short months I'd spent with Ario, I'd learned that for whatever reason, it was difficult for him to show gratitude, so when he finally said thanks, I cherished it like a gem.

"We all make decisions," I said.

"I made the wrong one."

"It's part of growing up."

Life is full of regrets. That's a fact. Regrets come whenever there's a decision to be made. When you have no choice, you don't have the luxury of having regrets. We make choices every day, as trivial as what we'd like to have for dinner. Maybe we'll regret it if we get food poisoning. But those who don't get a say on what to eat for dinner don't have the luxury of having regrets. They can, however, have regrets on the choices they made that put them in the situation where they no longer have dinner choices.

"You've never really told me why you fell in love with your husband."

"I don't know," Ario said. "I suppose because we connected. He critiqued my paintings. I critiqued his sculptures. We bonded over trips to galleries and museums, over obscure art films. He's intelligent and knowledgeable. You can ask him anything about art and he'll tell you the answer."

I sneaked a glance at Ario. He was smiling.

"Well," I said, "The Nurse got what he wanted."

"What?" Ario asked.

"He's now officially the guy from 'I know a guy who knew this guy.'"

Ario chuckled. "I wish him nothing but happiness. He deserves it."

We all do.

WHEN NOT WHY

Sylvia Plath, in her grief and madness, once said that when we gave someone our whole heart and he didn't want it, we could not take it back. It was gone forever.

She's right. We cannot take our heart back when we've given it fully to someone who doesn't want it. But unlike the heart, memories stay with us forever, whether joyous, painful or both. But it is possible for a new memory to invade a box that has long been possessed by other memories and force the old ones out.

Ario and I knew the exact moment we became really, fully aware that we loved our husbands.

In my case, it happened when I was binge-watching *Futurama* on Netflix and I finally came to "Meanwhile," that last episode where, due to a time-travelling mishap, Leela and Fry are the only people (and things) who aren't frozen in place. So they get married, travel the world together, walk on seas together, all while Chopin's aptly titled "Tristesse" plays in the background. In the end, Fry asks Leela if she could, would she do it all over again, and Leela answers yes. I thought of The Musician during the whole episode. Two years after we'd met for the first time, I watched it again and it still made me cry and think of him.

A similar thing happened to Ario, but it was more memory-based. The thought of The Sculptor also blocked a constant barrage of memories of his Voldemort. He was walking down Berkeley's College Ave from Rockridge BART Station after a party when he realized that during the walk, he was thinking of The Sculptor, of Los Angeles, of the comfortably cold art room in The Sculptor's house (the mallet incident hadn't happened yet). For Ario, College Ave used to be the street where he'd done the walk of shame from the BART station to his apartment that day when Voldemort told him he couldn't handle his complexity anymore. But The Sculptor, or rather, the fresh memory of The Sculptor, scooped out and replaced the frozen images of the terrible break up in that memory box labeled "Walking Home on College Ave" and filled it with a new one that was vibrant and jubilant and ripe with possibilities.

MALIBU BOYS

It took me at least a minute to drive from the enormous gates to the front door of the Malibu mansion where Jaya lived. He was waving to me as though he was just about to embark on the *Titanic*.

"Hey, you!" Jaya said. "*Macet ga*?" He wore yellow short shorts and an Anna from *Frozen* racerback tank top. His boyfriend, The Model, stood towering next to him, in a loose white sleeveless top and board shorts and his signature aviator sunglasses.

"*Macet banget, kayak* Jakarta," I said, complaining about the traffic and comparing it to Jakarta. It took me almost two hours to get there because of rush-hour traffic jams and construction. I was booked to do a sunset shoot on the beach with The Model, and then we'd move into the house for some intimate ones with both of them. Jaya's husband was out of town.

"Love your shirt," I said.

"Thanks! My Kristoff bought me this," Jaya beamed at The Model. "Want something to drink? We've a full bar."

"My baby makes awesome drinks," The Model cupped Jaya's butt. I had to remind myself that things would be even more intimate than that during the shoot.

"No. But I have lights and stuff in the car. Do you have someone who can help me carry those?"

"I'll do it," Jaya said. "And big guy here can help."

"No. That's okay. I can handle it." I never let my clients

carry my equipment. Even when I need help. When I do free work with models, I ask them to help me carry my stuff when I'm overwhelmed, but I always try not to.

It was already six in the evening and the sun would set in about thirty minutes, so we decided to do the sunset shoot with The Model first.

"Geez," I said as I was led inside the house, amazed by the spaciousness. Light cream marble floors with vases full of flowers. It looked like a house that was made to host parties. It was a dream house, at least for photoshoots.

"I thought your house in Jakarta looked like this," Jaya said.

"Not even remotely. My parents grew up poor, so they saved a lot and don't like to show off. My siblings and I don't even have AC in our rooms."

We walked past an Asian man about my age wearing a black and white uniform. He looked Pacific Islander.

"Hi," I said to him. He smiled and nodded and walked away.

"Who's that?" I asked Jaya.

"Our butler," he said.

"Indonesian?"

"Filipino."

Behind the tall glass doors was the beach. Jaya opened the doors and the breeze kissed my face. The waves were small and almost silent even as they crashed onto the sands.

"Go change," Jaya said to The Model. Moments later, he emerged in white briefs. "Hottie." They kissed. But Jaya suddenly pushed The Model away. "You should start."

We climbed down the stairs to the beach. From the corner of my eye, I saw the Filipino butler standing near the glass doors.

For a few minutes, Jaya helped pose The Model this way and that, but then his cellphone rang. He looked at the screen a few seconds before answering it and left us. The Model and I looked at each other and we decided to wait for Jaya. We saw him walk back to us and I thought we were going to resume the shoot.

"Sorry, guys, I have to take this," Jaya said and walked away again.

But the sun was at a perfect angle and I really didn't want to go home for nothing and drive back to Malibu for another shoot, so I told The Model that we should continue. He agreed and I set up my lights.

We wrapped the session when the sun had completely disappeared, but Jaya still hadn't come back.

"I wonder where he is," I said as I broke down the light stands. The model shrugged, but his face looked worried. It lit up when I asked him how things were between the two of them.

"I'm really happy he's here," he said. "Even under this weird condition."

"You mean his green card marriage?" I asked.

"Yeah. I mean, every time we go out, I always want to give him nice things, buy him nice things, take him to nice places, but this is LA, and models like me are a dime a dozen."

"Don't say that," I said. "I think you're really gorgeous. Even by LA standards."

"Thanks, but I'm Asian. You know how racist the modelling industry is, especially in LA."

"I'm sure Jaya doesn't want you to buy him things you can't afford."

"That's what he always says. But I really want to be the provider, you know? He's been helping me a lot, and I was already in love with him even before I knew he was really kind."

"How?"

"I first saw him at the restaurant where I work at as a waiter. He was with his husband. Then he came alone once, twice, three times, and so I started talking to him."

"Did he say why he was alone?" I asked.

"His husband was away on a trip," The Model said. "And it was the only place he felt comfortable to go alone. And that broke my heart. Nobody that beautiful should be lonely."

I wanted to punch The Model's face so badly. Ario was right. Jaya was lucky.

"How long have you been together?"

"Our first kiss was on December fourteenth."

We were already on the mansion's porch that overlooked the beach. The Model had taken off his aviators and when the warm yellow porchlight hit his face, I saw his eyes for the first time. I realized how sad they were. They didn't look hollow or sullen. The eyelids weren't droopy. His pupils were pure black.

Ario told me that The Model had the eyes of those children in Margaret Keane's paintings. I could see that now.

"Maybe we should go look for Jaya," I said.

"Uh, you go ahead. I'm not exactly allowed to be in the house."

What? Then how are we going to do the other session?

"Right. Okay. I'll go look for him. He's probably in his room." But there were at least a hundred bedrooms in this house. I dialed Jaya's number.

BLEED

The Filipino butler told me that I would find Jaya in the room at the end of the hallway. On the third floor. They had a third floor. I was panting when I got there. Its tall doors were heavy matte white teak. I didn't understand why Jaya didn't rejoin us when he'd finished his call.

"Jaya?" I called from outside the doors.

No answer.

"Hey, you okay?"

Nothing.

I remembered the *Frozen* shirt that he wore so I knocked again and sang, "Do you wanna build a snowman?"

He giggled from inside and after a few seconds, the door clicked open. I couldn't believe it worked.

"Have you been crying?"

"*Masuk,*" Jaya said, and I came in.

Jaya's room was the size of a basketball court. It was a gaudy, Rococo style room. Even with the gigantic oversized bed, the room still looked ridiculously big. It had its own seating area with sofas and a fainting couch. Everything was very *Louis Quinze*.

"We can't do the shoot today," he said.

I could see red marks on his short shorts.

"Are you bleeding? Did something happen?"

I grabbed him. He didn't resist when I inspected him.

There were several cuts in his outer thigh near his right hip, each one was about two inches long. They weren't scrapes.

"Did you do this?" I asked.

Jaya didn't answer. I ran to the bathroom to try to find a medicine cabinet. I opened every drawer near the sink, but they were either empty or only had towels.

"Is there a bandage or something?"

"Yes," he said. I followed him to a white wooden vanity table. He took out a large self-adhesive wound pad. "I have to remember to cut smaller next time."

"There won't be a next time," I said. "You must never do this again. Please get help. Does your husband know?"

Jaya shook his head no.

"Your boyfriend? Does he know?"

Again, no.

He winced when I put the pad over the cuts.

"It started when I was seven. I was in the choir. I didn't know the songs and I was really nervous. I couldn't read music notes. The folder for the music sheets had metal hinges and I would open the hinges, press my palm down on the tips, and slide it along. It wasn't enough to make me bleed, but it helped ease my nervousness."

I tried to remember what I was doing when I was seven. It was the nineties. I remembered hanging out with my friends in the schoolyard talking about hover cars and robots that would be invented in the year 2000, the year I would turn seventeen. But I couldn't find anything that made me want to cut myself.

"When I found a job in Bali and had enough money to go to school, I no longer wanted to talk to my parents and my brothers and sisters. But every time I went through a heartbreak, every time I failed a test, I'd cut myself. It was a way to remind me of the pain when my family and kids at school used to beat me for being girly. Every cut reminded me that it could be worse, and that I'd gone through worse."

Among the periwinkle and navy blue waves on his forearms were keloid bumps. "Tattoos helped. It's like cutting, but with gorgeous results."

"But what about now? Why can't you just get more tattoos?" I asked.

"I can't. It's in the contract."

"What contract?"

"My marriage. He'll divorce me if I get a tattoo. I cut myself from time to time, whenever my husband flies away to work. But I haven't cut myself in months, not since I met my boyfriend. But that Filipino butler told on me about my boyfriend being inside the house and my husband called and threatened to divorce me."

I didn't understand.

"No, it wasn't about love," Jaya said. "He said I'd been flaunting my body too many times to too many men and that he had a reputation to maintain. He said he couldn't be married to a whore."

"But didn't you save his life?"

"I guess everyone has limits."

"Do you love your husband?" I asked.

"I don't know. He's nice. He's very nice. I didn't even care that he was old. I told myself, I could love him. I mean, it could be worse. I could end up like Ario."

"And do you love your boyfriend?"

"He's nice too. And very handsome. And young. And I want to grow old with him. But I'm afraid he thinks I want him to provide for me. I'm afraid that when he fails or when he thinks he's failed to provide me, it's going to hurt both of us. He's not like my other boyfriends. I can trust this one. He has never asked me for money. He's always the one buying us things."

I thought of The Pilot. We were twenty years apart. Jaya and his husband were forty years apart. I'd seen photos of Jaya's husband. He wasn't ugly, even for someone who was in his late sixties.

"Why are you still with your husband?"

"Why is any immigrant still with his husband?" Jaya asked and looked at me as though I didn't know the answer to one plus one. "This," he opened his arms. "All of this. I will inherit this if I behave. My boyfriend may not want it, but I do. I'm tired of being poor."

"But your boyfriend is poor," I said.

"But with him, I don't care. With him, I'm not afraid of doing lowly jobs, but I don't know what's going to happen if I get a divorce. What if the relationship with my boyfriend doesn't work? It's a bird in the hand, right? I don't know if I can get another green card. I can't afford a lawyer. I don't have cash. Everything is paid through credit cards and my husband checks every item. He's Jewish. And I don't want to go back to Indonesia. I can't."

I was about to suggest buying things using credit card, selling them on eBay, and putting the money into a private bank account.

"Go to school," I said. "Take night classes in photography, design, whatever. Get a cosmetology license, or a real estate license. Use the credit card to pay for classes, to pay for equipment. It's for school. He can't object to that."

"And when the three-year mark finally comes, I can do

whatever I want and I have skills to work and earn money and be with my boyfriend."

You can be with anyone who loves you, I thought, or you can also choose to be alone. But yes, your boyfriend really loves you.

"*Terima kasih*," Jaya hugged me.

"Listen," I said, "you really have to tell someone about this. Someone close. You have to at least tell your boyfriend so he can keep an eye on you."

"I already know," The Model said. He'd been standing by the door the whole time.

"What are you doing? You can't be in here," Jaya stood up.

"I don't care." The Model walked the long path from the door to the vanity table. It was so long that it felt almost anticlimactic. "Look, I love you and I know you love me and I know we're currently in a strange cosmic arrangement, but I can wait. I'll wait for you for as long as you want. I'll do anything you want but please stop cutting yourself. And I agree with him. We'll take night classes. You can get certified in mixology."

How could you say no to those black, Asian Keane eyes?

"I stopped cutting myself when we met," Jaya said to The Model. "Honest."

He kissed Jaya's hands.

"We can't do the shoot. We need to lie low."

"Anything you want, baby."

That night, after The Model and I had left, Jaya sat alone in his bed and texted his husband to say that he'd broken up with his boyfriend. Then he signed up for bartending school in Thousand Oaks.

THE INTERVIEW

"Raise your right hand," their hearing officer said, "do you swear that all the information you're about to give is true?"

The Magnate and Jaya both said yes. They were at the Federal Building. It was July, five months after they were married.

"Please be seated," the officer said. Their lawyer sat behind them. She'd warned them that this particular officer was not the laughing kind.

"I'm locked out of my account because there's a glitch in our system, so I can only make the decision by the end of today or tomorrow. However, I need to remind you that you are still under oath, so you have to give honest answer. If you don't understand the question, let me know and I will try to explain it to you."

Yes.

"And also, it's all right to correct the other's answer if you think the answer is incorrect, but you have to let the person I'm asking answer it first."

Again, yes.

"All right, let's begin," the officer turned to Jaya. "Where do you currently reside?"

The Magnate's house. He gave the officer the address.

"And how long have you been living there?"

"I moved in in January."

The officer asked The Magnate the same question.

"I've lived there since 1975," The Magnate said. "I own the property."

The next ones were basic and directed to both of them.

No, we were never married before. No, we don't have children.

Then back to Jaya.

No, I've never been arrested. No, nowhere in the world. No, I have no addiction to drugs or alcohol. No, there's no other person beside my spouse who's helping me get a permanent residence. No, I'm not a member of any organization or group that dislikes anyone because of race, religion, or political belief.

The officer asked them their current phone numbers. The Magnate gave his assistant's.

"So, where did you two meet?"

"In Bali. I was working at the hotel where he stayed," Jaya said.

"He saved my life," The Magnate said. "I had a heatstroke." He reached out to Jaya and they held hands.

"Have you met his family?" the officer asked The Magnate.

"No. He'd left his house years ago."

"My family didn't like me because I was feminine. I moved to Bali and haven't had contact with them for years. But he's met my friends."

Their lawyer stood up and presented the copies of their airplane tickets and hotel bills. "There are also photos of them in the scrapbook."

Jaya showed the officer the scrapbook that he had made. He'd made sure that they took a lot of photos together and with friends, to solidify the image that they'd been together long enough to actually be in a real relationship.

"That's me and my friends," Jaya said. The officer flipped the page. "That's him and his friends." Flip. "That's him shopping for fruits in a traditional market in Jakarta."

"He writes adorable things about himself in the scrapbook," The Magnate said. "Mostly in Indonesian. No one understands it."

"Well, I was the one who prepared it," Jaya said.

The officer chuckled.

"Who knew this job would be so entertaining when you started it, right?" their lawyer said.

"This is one of the few times," the officer said. "Usually it's very boring." Flip.

"That was one of those galas, ugh," Jaya said.

"You don't sound too happy," the officer said.

"Oh, I hated it." He never knew what to say to those people. The old ones were one or two generations different, and the young ones looked at him with derision, although he knew full well that they only inherited the wealth of their parents.

"I didn't know that," The Magnate said. "He's such a good actor."

"I just don't want to embarrass you in front of your friends," Jaya said. "I do like dressing up in the tuxedo."

"I told you," The Magnate said to the lawyer. "He's a real catch."

"A real sweetheart too," she said.

"Great," the officer printed a letter and gave copies to them and the lawyer. "Like I said, since the system is having a glitch, I still need to check several things. If there are issues, I will contact your lawyer."

They shook hands and their lawyer walked with them to the door.

"If this is approved, three years from now you can apply to be a citizen," she said.

"I can't wait," Jaya said.

She laughed. "That's the spirit," she said before joining her other clients, a straight binational couple who was due for an appointment in a few hours.

THE DEMONS OF INDONESIA #5:

LEADERS

In 2008, Jakarta was hit by two gruesome murder cases. A married man was mutilated by his gay lover and an older gay man was stabbed multiple times by a trick. For whatever reason, the Jakarta Police Department thought it was wise to monitor forty supported meeting places of gay people in order to stop more gay-related criminal activities. Then-chief of Jakarta PD, Adang Firman, was even quoted as saying that gays were deviants.

This isn't an uncommon view. And despite the Indonesian Health Department's handbook that was published in 1983 and then renewed in 1993 that clearly states that homosexuality is not a mental disorder, many political leaders, religious leaders, political parties, organizations, and even scholars and the media, still refer to homosexuality as a disorder or a deviant behavior. The current Indonesian president, Joko Widodo, has a reputation of being corrupt-free and tireless in working for Indonesians, most recently for implementing Kartu Indonesia Sehat (Healthy Indonesia Card), a program similar to Medicare in the US. His opponents mostly criticize his liberal viewpoint.

But even for Widodo, with his liberal view and his work for human rights, queer rights are probably not on the top level of his list of priorities. In September of 2014, The United

Nations Human Rights Council adopted a resolution for LGBT rights, although it is seen by many as only symbolic since it does not have enforcement capability. Its role is to simply ask the UN high commissioner to report LGBT abuses. Nevertheless, the resolution was won on a vote of 25-14, with seven abstentions. Indonesia was not one of the seven. Did our Indonesian representative voted for or against? Clue: we shared the same opinion with Pakistan, Saudi Arabia, and the Russian Federation.

This atrocity went unnoticed. To be fair, Widodo officially became president in October of 2014 and again, to be fair, he already had so much on his plate, namely fighting rampant poverty and corruption. But there were still no words from the new Indonesian minister of law and human rights.

SCARE

I was officially the ugliest patient at The Hollywood Men's Wellness Center. Everyone was so young and beautiful that it could very well be the waiting room of a porn audition. Among the copies of *Frontiers* magazine, there was a thin publication called *Life After 50* and Kim Cattrall was the cover girl. I decided to pick it up because I didn't bring a book and I didn't want to read about WeHo parties.

The clinic itself was solemn, like a church or a funeral home. The two television screens were on mute, and everyone either kept to himself or talked in a low voice. There was no music, almost no sound, except for the occasional shuffling of the feet on carpet, and the staff calling out numbers or names and explaining the general procedure from behind glass windows.

Ario had a scare earlier and phoned me about the incident. I asked The Musician what to do and he told me to take him to the Men's Wellness Center to get PEP treatment.

"Do you want me to come with you?" The Musician said.

"Better not. I'm not sure if he wants to see you. You know, in this condition."

Now Ario and I were sitting in the clinic's waiting room.

"The thing is, he has tattoos all over and was in jail for a time," Ario said. "In another world, in another life, in another instance, that could be really sexy."

I was there to get checked. I was tested recently for immigration purposes, but I thought why not. It was free.

"Just so you know, I'm blaming you. You were the one who told me to have sex with someone else."

"Well, I'm sorry, but you also should've known better and used more lube."

Two men came in. They both looked extremely alike, with short trimmed beards and plugged earlobes. One was wearing a tank top and I could see his tattooed arms. One of the tattoos was a handwriting that said "To Oliver, Love, Stevie Nicks." I couldn't decide whether it was the tackiest or the strangest thing I'd seen in a long time, and I'd lived in Los Angeles for almost a year. I'm a fan of her but why would you want to have that permanently scarred on your skin? Then I thought at least it wasn't Stevie Nicks' face.

"I've always wanted to go here and get checked," Ario said. "Since I don't know where my husband dips his dick."

"Where is he now?"

Ario shrugged.

"Are you worried?"

"Of being infected?" Ario said. "Somewhat. My first hook-up in years and the condom had to break. But I read that PEP has a high success rate. You?"

"I'm always worried," I said. I bought OraQuick during my promiscuous months in Berkeley two years ago after my best friend in Indonesia told me he was positive. "But I was negative the last time."

"What would you do if you were positive?"

"It's impossible."

"But if you were?"

"It's not like it's life threatening. I mean, it will be if you don't take care of it, but as long as you're medicated, you'll be fine."

"And you're okay with the drugs being tested on animals?"

"I'm not Linda McCartney, okay?" I said. "I'm not a saint. I don't eat meat or wear animal products or use makeup that's been tested on animals because I have a choice not to. But drugs, especially HIV drugs, are for survival."

"Fair enough," Ario said.

I swear, sometimes I really did want to hit Ario with a mallet. But I reminded myself, I wasn't the one with the scare. I wasn't the one who was potentially infected. The truth is, I didn't know what I would do if I got it. Two years before, I found blood in my ejaculation. The first time it happened, I didn't pay too much attention. Then it happened again, and again, and again. It wasn't a lot, maybe one or two drops, but it was enough to freak me out. I didn't experience pain when I ejaculated or urinated. My boys looked normal, no swelling, discharges, mucous, or anything that was a telltale sign of STDs. And I know I should've gone to a physician instead of Googling "blood in semen please help." But I didn't have insurance, and finding a solution on the Internet and buying Cranberry pills were far cheaper than going to the doctor. I never knew what really caused it, but as soon as I began taking the pills, there were no longer blood spots. From online articles about hematospermia, I concluded that it had to happen because my prostate was damaged from penetration. And because it wasn't contagious and I had it under control, I didn't feel the need to tell my partners. Sex went on per usual and my semen was blood-free.

But if I were to be infected with something contagious, I would have no other choice but to tell my partner. And as much as I try to downplay the severity of HIV, it still is not syphilis nor gonorrhea. HIV infection would change not only my life, but also my partner's, whether or not he is infected.

I was flipping the pages of *Life After 50* when my name was called. So much for finding out what Ms. Cattrall had to say about aging.

"Good luck," Ario said.

I thought of my close friend in Jakarta who's HIV positive. How I wished I'd been there to wish him good luck, but that probably would've been as futile as opening the refrigerator door in the middle of the night and reopening it two minutes later, hoping for some exciting meal to magically appear.

THERMOPYLAE

Everything began to spiral down the moment the Internist told him to get his blood checked for HIV infection.

You have a high monocyte level count, the Internist said.

He was only there to get answers about the stomachache that had been bothering him, but he did the HIV test anyway. The second doctor he saw when he picked up his test result two days later was a bored GP on duty who politely refused to answer his question about the meaning of the word "reactive" on the white paper.

I'm sorry, was all the GP said.

But he knew. He'd known. He'd Googled it. It's uncanny the things you learn on the Internet. And it was damning.

All those years of worrying about things like failing a class and not having good grades (he was a valedictorian) turned out to be just that: worries. Groundless worries. Those feelings of dying of failure or broken heart were also just worries. But this, of all things, was real.

He took two days off from work. It was unheard of. He needed work. He lived to work. To be busy and not have to think of other things but his job. But this one needed his full attention.

That day, after he called in sick, he spread himself thin on his bed, limbs outstretched. The white paper on one side, his laptop on the other. He was in a lying *trikonasana*, the star pose, but he didn't feel like one, so he curled into a fetus.

Philadelphia. Gia. The Hours. He reminded himself it was not AIDS. Not yet. He could be treated. The Internet said so.

Who was it? Who gave it to me? Does it matter?

The Internet helped him find a doctor. He called the number and made an appointment for the next day.

The hospital was near the place he used to meet his boyfriend, back when he had dreams and time, and they would go out to eat, watch a movie, or do things that people do on dates.

Was it him? It couldn't be him. We were always so careful. What is he up to these days now that we're no longer talking? Should I tell him?

It took him twenty minutes to find the building, then the ward. The hospital was massive. Its walls and corridors bore witness to decades of good news and bad news.

A nurse in hijab greeted him. He was asked to fill out a form, uncover his identity. He wasn't anonymous on file. Faceless, but not without a name. Then again, like billions of others, you can always find him on the Internet.

A healthy person's T-Cell count, the doctor said, should be between five hundred and twelve hundred. Yours is only three hundred.

Three hundred Spartan T-Cells fighting against an army. He imagined a cinematic battle being waged inside his body, but he knew who won. The history knew who won. You can look it up on the Internet if you don't know.

Don't worry, the doctor said. It can be managed. We've seen as few as nine T-Cells.

The doctor prescribed him some drugs, including one for his pneumonia. No raw eggs, no raw meat, no sashimi.

He loved sashimi.

Even as he was outside the doctor's office, he was still

waiting for him to say, Oh we made a mistake. You're actually healthy. Or, Why don't you do another test, tests like these are usually inaccurate. Or, Surprise, you're on candid camera!

But none of those things happened and he found himself crying in the arms of the nurse with the hijab.

You'll be fine, she said as she rubbed his heaving back. Her words melted the icy clinical and precise sentences that had come out of the doctor's mouth. She called him sweetie. She told him she'd seen patients with worse conditions survive.

He had nightmares from the first batch of medication. He couldn't remember what they were, but he always woke up in fear. Then it got worse. He had a headache that almost made him throw up, his skin was red and itchy all over, and his throat was swollen shut. It was public holiday, and he thought he was lucky because he didn't have to take a sick leave. He called the nurse and she met him near his house and took him to the doctor who changed the prescription.

The second batch of medication didn't give him side effects and he gradually became healthier, his T-Cell count became higher than the average person. He didn't even sneeze when everyone in the office got a cold.

And now that that part was over, he had to think of telling people close to him. He decided to tell his family: his mother and his sister. Over dinner. Then he must tell his close friend who was studying abroad. He would tell him the next time he was in Jakarta. They were Sally and Gillian Owens, the sisters from *Practical Magic*. He was Sally, the one who doesn't want to fall in love, and his friend was Gilly-bean, the serial lover. He wondered if they would one day fight the ghost of his friend's abusive ex, if they would grow old together in a house full of cats, if he would meet his true love who had one blue eye and one green, who flipped pancakes in the air, who would whistle his favorite song, who could ride a pony backward, and whose favorite shape was a star.

AMORE, MORE, ORE, RE

"Have you ever noticed that everyone is so attractive?" my friend said. We were sitting at a corner table in a restaurant in Jakarta. It was raining outside. Tropical rain that makes the air moist and cold.

"Look who's talking," I said. I was home for the summer holiday.

He poured jasmine tea into my cup. "I've something to tell you," he said.

"What?" I reached over the table, past the empty plates, and grabbed the white bone china. "Oh my God. You have a boyfriend? Finally!"

He shook his head. "No, silly."

"You're pregnant! That's why you're glowing."

He shook his head again. "I wish."

"Then what is it?" I was eyeing a Caucasian and his bulging biceps who was sitting across from us. "So?" I looked at my friend again. He was smiling. I thought it was going to be something good, something positive. Maybe a job promotion. "Are you sure it's not a boyfriend?"

"I'm HIV-positive," he said.

The white china cup burned my palms and I put it down on the marble table. My friend was dead right in front of me. I reached over to hand him the white paper napkins.

"But don't worry, I'm fine," he said and took the napkins to wipe his tears. "I mean, I'm on meds. I just need to take good care of myself. The meds help place the virus under control."

The virus. I'd checked myself the year before when I was visiting The Baker in Bali. I was "nonreactive." Why do they say HIV-positive when someone has the virus? It's not like it's a good thing, it's not like the answer is a positive yes, I do want to marry you or a positive yes, I'm pregnant. Maybe I should write it with a capital V. The Virus. Give it a funny name, a character. Find a flint of gold or diamond on its ugly armor and try to write it in a more positive way so that it's more fleshed-out, more three-dimensional. There you go. Another positive and negative battle of balance.

"Please don't cry. It's not AIDS," he said. The damn paper napkins were the kind that was good for absorbing grease, not water. "There's a support group for positive Indonesians," he silently acknowledged the three-letter acronym. "One of the members wrote to me, 'Don't overwhelm yourself with information on the Internet. The more you read, the more frustrating and depressing it gets.' And he's right. I just go to my doctor, do routine check-ups, ask him what food or drink I'm allowed to take. I'm fine. And the drugs here are free."

A family walked in and sat at a table to my right. A young couple, a little girl in a pink dress, a baby in a carriage, an older woman whom I deduced as an in-law of either the man or the woman. The three adults opened the menu. The father pointed at the pictures on the menu to the little girl on his lap. The rain outside had stopped.

I knew my friend had been battling the same questions. Why now? Why me? And I knew it was more unfair for him than for me, so I got up and sat next to him and held him, letting him rest his lovely bald head on my shoulder.

I wanted to say I'm here. I'm here. Please stop crying,

or don't stop crying, or thank you for crying in front of me, next to me, with me, in my arms, for wetting my shirt, for being vulnerable. Yes, thank you for being vulnerable and sharing this with me, only with me, it means a lot to me. If only it were some better news, something positive in every sense of the word, of a loving boyfriend perhaps, or a job promotion that you very well deserve, or a lottery victory. I'd be jealous, I'd be insanely jealous, but I'd still be happy for you. And yes, I'm here. Like you are always there for me. Remember New Year's Eve eleven years ago? Our first real-life New Year? We were supposed to go to a get-together that our friend and his boyfriend had invited us to. We arrived at the hotel, but I realized I'd lost my wallet and you and I spent the better part of the evening searching for it, even going back to the church where I'd attended New Year's Eve mass. My mother was as exasperated as I was. The wallet had everything: my driver's license, my college ID card, debit cards, not really that much money, but still, getting them replaced would be a pain. You and I ended up staying at my house, watching *Alien* and *Aliens*, two of our favorite movies, and eating strawberry ice cream on toast. It was an impromptu pajama party in my non-AC room, as firecrackers and fireworks exploded outside and terrorized my poor cats. In the morning, when your taxi arrived, you told me I snored and I told you you drooled. We laughed and I decided it was the best New Year's Eve ever. My mother loves you. She always says, "I love him. He's a good kid." I'm jealous, but I couldn't agree more. You're always there. Unlike the times when I ignored your messages over Internet messenger because I was busy doing trivial things. But I'm here now.

"This is why I didn't come to your dance recital," he said. "I was worried that I couldn't drink inside the auditorium and couldn't take my pills."

I held him still. I didn't want to let this beautiful man slip away from me.

"I'm really, really glad I didn't wear my eyeliner and mascara today," I said, and I cursed. This is why I don't go to funerals. Or weddings. Or baby showers. I always manage to say the stupidest things and it's not like I haven't thought them over. No. I'm too self-conscious, too self-aware, too self-important not to care about what I say, what I do, what I wear, how I look, walk, behave. And I thought for fuck's sake why couldn't I stop thinking of myself? Of how this would affect my life? Always me, me, me. What made me so entitled? So privileged? Never a valedictorian, almost flunked high school, and I was certainly not the one who was looking at one of the world's most loathed and feared viruses in the eyes and flipping the bird as it choked him. But it made my friend laugh, and his laugh made me laugh, and I realized perhaps I needed it more than he did, the assurance of laughter. But it wasn't that easy, was it? It stopped being that easy five minutes ago.

"Sometimes," he said, "sometimes I wonder if I could pinpoint the moment I made that mistake, you know? Just to know when and with whom. And warn my younger self."

But it would remain a mystery, would it? I thought of my own liaisons. I was very, very lucky indeed. Very lucky to inherit my mother's anxiety and paranoia. Very lucky to have this scarred body, this unevenly colored skin, this flat ass, these crooked teeth, because they stunted my confidence and made me live quite a long, sexless life. I'd had my glory-whorey days, yes, but I was still in the safe zone. But for how long? How long would this luck hold?

And there I went again. Me, me, me again. What did Plath write? Oh, yes. The "old brag of my heart: I am, I am, I am." Old brag indeed.

"Did you know that Singapore banned positive tourists?"

"No!" I said. "How could they? How could they tell?" I reached over the table and poured jasmine tea into our cups. It was still warm, but there was no longer steam.

"The pills. They check the pills. They're blacklisted. I've bought round-trip tickets for a weekend in Singapore. I guess I'll have to let them go."

"Those bastards," I said. "But how would they know? You could put them in the checked baggage." Either way, it was score one for Indonesia. We're decidedly and tangibly more tolerant than the oh-so-superior Singapore, at least to HIV-positive visitors.

But my friend just shrugged and chuckled and the sky had become grey again and the monsoon rain started again and it mercilessly soaked the trees, and the cars and the people and made the streets and the pavements slick and slippery again.

We sipped our jasmine tea side by side and I felt weak and tired and bent as though we'd aged so much in mere minutes. I wanted to wave the prying eyes of our neighbors away. Nothing to see here, people. Just two old friends sipping tea.

"You know what?" he said, his brush-stroke thin eyes red and swollen, perhaps as red and as swollen as mine were.

"What?"

"We need sugar." His smile bloomed on those naturally pink lips on his smooth face.

"Damn right." I dabbed the useless paper napkin on my eyes and kissed his flawless, drenched cheek. "Let's go get some fucking cakes."

MIDDLE FINGER

I was led to a well-lit room and asked to sit. My nurse was a soft-spoken gentleman in his early thirties. He didn't wear scrubs, but jeans and shirt with his ID badge tagged on the pocket over his heart. He asked me to confirm my birthdate.

"You're here for the rapid test?"

I nodded. I didn't know what kind of test I needed, but I told the front desk I'd like to get my HIV status checked.

He asked me a series of questions about my sexual history.

Yes, I bottom only. No, I don't do drugs. Yes, I drink occasionally. No, I'm not a porn performer. No, I'm not an escort. No, I don't use poppers.

On the table were several small vials and contraptions. He asked me which hand I used the least. It was my left one.

"Flip me." He opened the vial with the yellow cap and took out a needle with a tiny container.

"Excuse me?"

"I need to prick your middle finger, so I want you to flip me."

Ah.

So I did.

He held my middle finger, rubbed it with a cotton ball swabbed with alcohol, and pricked its side near the top. The blood was neatly collected inside the container. He opened the vial with the red cap and put some drops of blood in it.

He replaced the cap, shook the vial, and dumped the content into a tiny white bowl. He opened the vial with the blue cap and poured the solution into the bowl. The blood and the solution mixture first started blue, but after a little while turned white (or maybe transparent, but I couldn't tell). Lastly, he opened the vial with the black cap and poured another solution into the mixture. It remained white (or transparent).

"Negative," he said.

I exhaled.

"Would you like to have a printed proof?"

"Yes, please. Can I ask something?"

"Sure."

"What do poppers have to do with sexual health?" I said.

"It can cause brain damage. Why?"

"Dammit."

"Why?" he said.

"Nothing. I should've encouraged my ex to use them more often."

He laughed and took out a small sheet of blue paper.

"Can I ask another question?"

"Go ahead," he said.

"Why the middle finger?"

"Oh, just a personal preference. To me, it's the most convenient. The thumb is not very flexible and you can't hold it out like other fingers; the index finger is the most used so it's usually callused on the side or it can be uncomfortable even if it's just a little prick; the ring finger can't be extended too much; and the pinky is simply too small."

You learn something every day.

But still, it could be more poetic. It could be like figuratively giving the bird to HIV.

I came out with a piece of white paper. My name was on it, along with a sticker from the rapid test pack, date of test, and a statement saying I was HIV-negative. Ario received a similar piece of paper. He was in the clear. And so we waited for him to get his initial PEP drugs.

GHOSTS

Singapore isn't only unfriendly to HIV-positive travelers. In the wake of SCOTUS' support of gay marriage, The Prime Minister of Singapore, Lee Hsien Loong, declared that Singapore wasn't ready for it. The country still illegalizes gay sex between men (but not between women). Lee warns gay groups not to push their agenda because there will be a strong pushback and that this issue is not something that can be discussed. Gay people are still required to enlist in their armed or police forces, although with limited duties.

A door away, the Prime Minister of Malaysia, Najib Razak, doesn't mince words and likens queers to—wait for it—ISIS. Yes. The same terrorist group that murders gay people. Razak said, "Such [extremist and liberal] groups [that] includes [sic] the Islamic State (IS) and Lesbian, Gay, Bisexual and Transgender community (LGBT) are targeting the younger generation to spread their ideologies—and it seems like they have managed to influence them."

Malaysia considers transgenderism and gay sex illegal.

In Indonesia, only Aceh, the Islamic province with its sharia law, declares gay sex illegal and demands public caning of up to one hundred lashes for people who get caught doing it. Except for that one backward province, there's no Indonesian law that says gay sex is either legal or illegal. This is a double-edged sword. For some, it's a relief, despite quite the few instances of people and organizations shouting for an action to stop us, as though there were a special button that we could use to not be gay or trans.

For others, this is bad news. We can still be fired or denied service because there's no law in Indonesia that governs discrimination based on sexual orientation and gender identity. There's no law in Indonesia that deals with hate crimes based on sexual orientation and gender identity. It's a cruel irony that the reason why the current President Widodo hasn't given more consideration on MUI's *fatwa* for capital punishment for gays is probably because he needs allies like the US and Europe to think he's progressive while at the same time, he needs support from Muslims (87.2% of total 250 million, making Indonesia the country with the largest Muslim population, 99% are Sunnis).

Queer Indonesians are still expected to be tolerant, to lie low, to pay taxes, to keep spending their hard-earned money and buy Indonesian products or at least buy nonlocal products in Indonesia and not go to neighboring, wealthier countries such as Singapore or Malaysia.

The fact that this is still a "don't ask, don't tell" situation is because some of us fear every single day that if we do bring up this sleeper issue, we'll face a backlash so bad that we'll end up destroying whatever shred of tolerance of queers is left in Indonesia. As humans, we too are capable of love and we long to be with the one we love, the one who also loves us. An acceptance in the form of legalization of gay marriage is one of the essential steps to prove that we can lead a life free from fear. Every creature has the right to love and to live without fear, but those rights are denied from us. We are not recognized. We are merely ghosts, floating and coasting by, acknowledged but invisible. We are used to create sensational headlines, and then we are exorcised and banished to our own mysterious paths and existence that sometimes cross with those who are lucky enough to be alive.

Maybe this is why some of us chose to flee. Maybe this is why some of us chose to abandon the people we love. We just want to be considered humans.

YOU CAN HAVE HIM

"I can't do this anymore," Ario said.

They were in The Sculptor's workroom. The place smelled like clay and rust and sex. A week before, he'd witnessed The Sculptor fuck one of his models again. He had let it happen five too many times, but this time, it wasn't the typicality or the predictability of the act that bothered him. He heard The Sculptor tell the model that he loved him. Not his lips, not his cock, not his ass, but him. He loved him. And The Sculptor's laughter as the model told him something Ario couldn't decipher. It was genuine, sweet, fresh, unburdened. Ario had never heard him laugh like that. And he had been prepared should this ever happen. For the last month, Ario had spent hundreds of dollars secretly packing and sending his books, shoes, knick-knacks, trinkets, and most of his clothes to Indonesia. The rest he either sold online or gave away. All that was left—crucial items he would need if things were to get better, if he were to stay, if they were to talk things out, reach an agreement—were stuffed inside a dirty lavender suitcase and a generic black backpack.

"I'm flying back to Jakarta tomorrow." The decision was abrupt and absolute. "The divorce papers will come soon. You can sign or not sign. The Indonesian government doesn't recognize our marriage anyway. As far as they're concerned, I'm not married. But it doesn't matter."

"You have like what? A year and a half to be a US citizen?" The Sculptor said.

One year, four months, and twenty-eight days, Ario thought. "It doesn't matter."

"Then what? What will you come home to in Jakarta? Muslims with loudspeakers waking you up at three in the morning? People staring at you for your fashion sense and the way you talk? You know there are too many crazy people ruling your country. You're too gay to live there. You won't be safe."

What do you know about Indonesia? Nothing. You were only there once, for two weeks, and you spent most of it in Bali.

"I'd rather be unsafe at home than be safe here," Ario said.

"Where will you be staying tonight?"

"A motel."

"You're not even going to tell me which one?"

Ario shook his head. "My life is no longer of your concern. And I know it hasn't been for the last ten months."

"Fuck you. That's untrue and unfair. I let you live here. I bought you food. I cooked for you and cleaned for you and let you drive my car."

"Now you won't have to worry about those things."

What have you told that kid, Ario wanted to ask. Did you tell him sweet words? Did you give him small, soft kisses on the nape of his neck?

"I love you," Ario said. The Sculptor didn't say anything. But for the first time in a long time, he looked at Ario. And Ario saw traces of tenderness, the same tenderness one would give a dying stranger. He told The Sculptor he didn't want to be a burden. He didn't have a job. Not really. He couldn't have his own apartment. He'd cluttered The Sculptor's house. He saw Ario lounging about, starting projects and not finishing them, leading a true Bohemian life, on a perpetual holiday. The house smelt like oil paint and turpentine. Piles of unfinished paintings. And how many easels could one person possibly need? And he understood why The Sculptor was short with him. He was an eyesore and he did absolutely nothing to improve the situation.

"You deserve better," Ario said. "We tried, my God, we tried, but we had a good run, didn't we?"

"What are you going to tell your parents? Your friends?"

"That it didn't work. And I'm going to leave it at that."

Ario took one last look around the room. At the mounds of clay, the metal tools, the lewd, headless, amputated sculptures. At a ten-inch-by-ten-inch area on the cement floor that had cracked when The Sculptor threw the mallet. Ario wondered if The Sculptor had noticed that Ario's belongings had been absent these past weeks. Behind the box of dozens of warped and bent jars and vessels, he saw the black tube that contained the mandala painting he'd made for The Sculptor. A mandala is a universe. That was why he painted that and gave it to The Sculptor. He was Ario's universe. Or at least he used to be. Ario wanted to ask if he could take it, but he decided to leave something, a mark, a tangible evidence of his presence in this house, in The Sculptor's life.

Ario's phone buzzed.

"My ride is here."

And that was it.

DRUNK

"Listen," The Sculptor said, "are you really interested in the truth?"

"What truth?" I asked. We were on the phone. He called to tell me that Ario had left him and asked if he was with me. I didn't even know that Ario had left.

"He fucked my best friend," The Sculptor said. "Did he tell you that?"

"No," I said.

"One night, he was drunk, I mean, really drunk. And out of the blue, he said he wished I'd been a better fuck, like my friend."

I didn't know what to say.

"Ario told me you were in an open relationship, and that was difficult for him."

"That doesn't mean he should fuck my friends. If he had better judgment, he would know that it was off-limits."

"All's fair in open relationships," I said. "You should know this. You were the one who wanted it."

I realized that remark might have cost me a photo gig or two, but it needed to be said and it shut him up.

The affair happened once, two years ago. The Sculptor learned about it a year later, a few months after they'd been married.

"That was a long time to forgive and move on," I said.

"He became weird after that. We could no longer talk like a normal couple. Look, I know you're his close friend . . ."

"I wouldn't go that far."

"Whatever. I just thought you should know."

I know. I felt betrayed too.

TOM BRADLEY

INTERNATIONAL TERMINAL

It was, as always, a pain to get to Tom Bradley International Terminal at LAX. And it was, as always, a pain to say goodbye.

The last time I said goodbye at LAX was to my mother, father, and brother, and it was quite unceremonious. The Musician and I had to hurry back to the car because an officer told us to move it. There were no tears because there was no time for tears. I left them after I paid for a cart (what a ghastly concept, airport carts should be free). Through the rearview mirror, I saw three stranded Asians, two of them late sexagenarians, one of them intellectually disabled, to fend for their lives through throngs of cranky people who were going to endure the routine checks, the long waits, and the flight itself.

But that day I chose to park and walk with Ario until he was ready to wait in the boarding lounge. He'd texted me to come pick him up and drive him to LAX, and he'd wanted to say a proper *adieu*.

"My mom was so ecstatic to hear that I was going home for good that she bought me a first class ticket. Not business class. Not some bullshit premium economy class. First class," Ario said. "One way, thank God."

"What's the first thing you're going to do when you arrive in Jakarta?"

"First, I'm going to buy a dozen packs of Djarum." He opened his pack of cigarettes and lit the last one. "This is for you," he handed me the empty pack.

"Gee, thanks," I said.

"Look on the back."

I flipped it over and saw that it was covered with a drawing of a peacock.

"It's Erté. Well, ish. His was always so elegant. Chic. Very art deco."

"But it's all pink and black. Is this glitter gel?" Some of the glitter was already falling off, on my fingers, my jeans, the car mat.

"Well, 'elegant' and 'chic' don't really describe you, but 'morbid' does. And I added a touch of fagginess to it too."

"Thank you," I smiled. "I like it."

"It's a Maison d'Ario original. Here, I'll sign it. It may be worth something one day. And you can sell it when you're broke." He actually took out a gold Sharpie from his backpack and signed his name on the front. Hearts and all. "You're welcome."

"You didn't tell me that you had sex with your husband's friend," I said as we walked out of the car.

Ario looked at me. I couldn't decode his expression. He'd become good at that.

"Who told you that?"

"Your husband called me last night."

"He's not my husband," Ario flicked his wrist. There was a light trail of dark tobacco droppings and a white screen of smoke.

"You didn't tell me," I said.

"Why should I? It's none of your business."

"It would've helped me understand your relationship."

"So you won't make the same mistake?" Ario asked, but I felt it was more of an accusation.

"I need to know both sides of the story," I said.

"You have his number. Go ahead and ask him."

"He just said I should know this side of you, and maybe that was why your marriage crumbled."

"He never gave us a chance to work things out. I thought that I could give him time and space to recuperate. I may have given him too much time and space."

"Why didn't you tell me?" I asked.

"Because it was painful, okay?" Ario said. He semi-shouted a barrage of French cuss words. Some people glanced at us.

I didn't want to believe him. I realized there was so much that I didn't know about Ario. But I also knew that when something greatly affects us, we either don't talk about it or can't stop talking about it. There's a sense of purge when you talk about it at length, whether to a friend or to a paid professional. In writing, baring the truth can hurt you, and there is no such thing as objective truth when it comes to memories. There is no such thing as truth, period, when it comes to memories. Everything that makes us who we are—our socio-economic backgrounds, our upbringing, our race, our genes—is responsible for shaping the way we view memories and project them.

But pain, as subjective as it is, is a real feeling. And I believed Ario when he said he didn't talk about it because it was too much.

"Do you remember that time we were at The Abbey, and I didn't answer when you asked me that if I were American, would I marry my husband?"

Ario nodded. "What about it?"

"I didn't answer not because I wouldn't want to marry him, but because it took me a long time to know the answer."

"And?"

"Now I have it. And I'm certain of it. The answer is yes, I would do it."

Ario grasped both of my shoulders. I could smell the cigarette and feel its heat on my right cheek.

"Get out of here," he said. "Get out while you still can."

A family of four loaded a cart with eight suitcases. Ario rolled his eyes and let go of my shoulders.

"What about your PEP?" I said.

"It's done," Ario said. "I'm all clear."

"What about The Nurse?"

"What about him?"

"Can't you contact him?"

"He married the other guy two months ago. The Filipino he's been with ever since I left him."

I didn't know what to say.

"I know. It's all very Nijinsky." Ario waved his hand again and exhaled translucent white smoke out of his mouth.

I didn't know who that was.

"Well, he's too young for me anyways. And he can't control his drinking. So . . . Will you write me?"

"Only if you promise to visit."

"Oh, darling, I'm never going to set foot in this country ever again."

"Please don't go," I said.

Ario took out his green card from his wallet. He pinched one edge and placed the other on top of his lighter.

"No."

The fire melted the card. It was so slow that I felt as

though I was watching snails racing. After a while, one half of the card began to flap, like wet toilet paper.

"And I say: please come with me to Indonesia. Your family is waiting for you there. And your friends. And your bloody cats."

Everything was noisy and moving. An orchestra of commotions. The laughter, the silence, the words of advice. The embraces, the kisses, the hellos and goodbyes. The sounds and sights of departure gates everywhere are identical. Yearning is a universal feeling.

"One day," I said.

Ario tossed the melted card into a trashcan. "You know, I feel bad for not telling the Other Boy that it might be cyclical."

"Cyclical?"

"My husband, well, hopefully soon to be ex-husband, left his boyfriend to marry me. People who do that are bound to repeat the same pattern. Over and over again. Hopefully that little tart won't take it too badly."

But what does that mean about me? I thought. I'm also guilty of leaving lovers.

Ario stubbed out his cigarette.

"Come on," he hooked my arm in his and exhaled his last cigarette smoke in the US. Then he gestured at me to take his lavender suitcase. "I can't wait to stroll through these peasants and finally fly first class."

IT'S HERE

My permanent resident card arrived with a congratulatory letter. It's plastic, thicker than a regular credit card. The back is cowrie shell white slashed by a thick dark magnetic strip. The front is green. The color of go. The color of lush forest leaves. Of emerald and jade. Of malice and radioactivity. Of the lights coming out of Minas Morgul, where the Witch-king of Angmar resides and Sauron breeds his army. Of the Borg in Star Trek universe, the malevolent, powerful band of collective species that always seeks to forcefully assimilate other species, therefore adding their knowledge and information into their collective hive mind.

The card bears my name, curly signature, thumbprint, date of birth, sex, date of my residence, date of card expiration, and a photo of me with a weird haircut, looking way too happy. It also has my category: CR6. Spouse of American citizen.

CR stands for Conditional Residency, which means I still have to prove that I didn't marry as a shortcut to be a citizen. I can apply to remove this condition by filing a form with my husband within ninety days before the expiration date of my card, which is exactly two years after the date of my conditional residency. I will lose my conditional resident status and be deported if I don't do this. I can apply to waive the joint filing requirement if my US-citizen husband and I have legally separated, or if I've been abused by him. However, to be able to stay in the US, I must prove that going back to Indonesia would be dangerous.

On the top left corner of the card is a shimmering copper head of the bald eagle. The head of the Statue of Liberty is prominently displayed on the card.

There's a sonnet called "The New Colossus" by Emma Lazarus. It was written one hundred years before I was born. Lazarus wrote the poem for a fundraiser auction to gather money to build the Statue of Liberty's pedestal. However, after the auction, the poem was forgotten. Lazarus' friends campaigned to have the sonnet memorialized. The campaign was a success and in 1903, a bronze plaque bearing the sonnet was mounted inside the statue's pedestal.

The tenth and eleventh lines of the sonnet read, "Give me your tired, your poor, your huddled masses yearning to breathe free."

THE WOMAN AND THE MAN IN THE LIVING ROOM

The woman and the man sit in their living room as they watch the debate on television. It's about politics, it's about religion, it's about people. People like their son.

A week after they returned to Indonesia from visiting their son and his husband in the US, its Supreme Court ruled that gay marriage must be legalized in all states. And since the country has the strongest global presence, this decision affected all corners of the world, including theirs.

They watch as rows after rows of university students in the audience yell no when the host asks if they agree with gay marriage in their country. The host is an ally. He's on their side. But the students, with their proud yellow jackets, are not. Their own alma mater. They met there when she was a student and he was assistant lecturer. Their son also went there, continuing the tradition.

She clicks her tongue. He shakes his head.

Unbelievable, he says.

Those people, she says.

Deviants, predators, but they can be cured if they accept God, says a speaker, an old woman. She wears a hijab. The woman in the living room has relatives who wear hijab. Her dear sister-in-law also wears hijab. And this dear sister-in-law never says anything about her son.

Do you remember when he first came into our lives? the woman in the living room asks the man. Such beautiful joy. So intelligent.

So rebellious, the man says, but with amused tenderness. The man and the son fought, but their explosive disagreements are now parts of their memory, their learning process, of him being a parent and of his son growing up. The man used to be so strong, so towering. He could pin his son down on the floor during tantrums.

The woman and the man have always known about their son.

The man used to think, What if I'd spent more time with him?

While the woman wondered, What if I'd spent less?

The children of their friends, of their sisters and brothers lead normal lives. Those children grew up, got married, started a family of their own, produce grandchildren for their parents.

Why can't we? they used to ask their god.

A shy, unmarried daughter, an intellectually handicapped son, and their youngest just has to be a flaming homosexual.

Why can't we have grandchildren too?

A house of misfits. Their bloodline ends there. Three strikes, they're out.

Do you remember when he lost his little lion doll? the woman asks. You went looking all over for it.

It was raining too, the man says. How old was he? Six? Seven?

Ten, the woman says.

She stood by, holding their crying son as the man searched for it. He came back, empty-handed, drenched, and heroic. The son now has another doll. A ginger kitten that travels all over the world with him. They've been together for more than twenty years.

Deviants, sinners, pedophiles. The debate continues. The allies aren't allowed to speak. The bigots talk over them, cut their sentences. It's a blood bath. We can't win.

For Pete's sake, let them speak, the man in the living room says.

He was the first one to accept his son. It took her longer.

Do you remember when he used to bring home kittens? the woman asks.

Two of those kittens, now cats, are still there. One of them is curled up against the woman's feet, missing his human every day.

I didn't even know I liked cats, the man says.

He's writing a book, the woman says. I wonder if he can use a fake name.

Why? the man asks.

What if he can't come back here? the woman asks. What if I can't see him again because he's not permitted to visit us here? You remember what those people did to that lesbian Canadian writer when she came here.

But he has to use his real name, the man says. He must.

Why? the woman asks.

Because that's his identity, the man says. That's what he is. That's who he is. He can't write in fear.

There are hundreds of people in that television studio. There are hundreds of millions of people in their country. Surely not every one of them opposes gay marriage, or thinks that gays are vile? Surely some must have gay friends or gay children?

Surely we're not the only parents with a gay child? How do others cope? If they cope at all?

The fact is, the man in the living room says, these scared and small people do indeed represent our country. It's a good thing our son is not here.

But they don't know that some nights, their son would cry and yearn to be with them, although it would mean he'd also be among those scared and small people.

The debate ends. The victors will go back to their homes and resume their lives, their heads and chests swell with pride because once again they've shouted to the world that their god will smite down these deviants. And shouting always works. The rest? Well, they lick their wounds and limp their ways back into silence and darkness. Their friends and allies will greet them and hug them and pat their backs and say, You've done your best. But there will be an awkward post-consolation silence and someone amongst them will ask if they will still be alive when their beloved country finally understands that they are also humans.

The woman and the man are glad their son is not there to witness this, to witness his own people condemning him, calling him a criminal, forcing him to follow their god and their prophet, doubting his humanity and his sanity, dissecting him, chewing him and spitting him out.

It could be worse, the man says. We could have a confident, outgoing daughter who'd party every night. We could have a son with normal intelligence and he could be a drug addict or a drunk. We could have a straight son and he'd abuse women.

Or, the man continues, they could all turn out average,

and we'd live and die as average people, never knowing what it means to have special children.

I don't think I'd want that, the woman says.

I don't either, the man says.

No regrets, the woman says.

No regrets, the man says.

LIMBO (THIS COULD BE OUR STONEWALL)

In January of 2016, *Republika*, a nation-wide Indonesian Muslim newspaper, released an article that featured a baiting headline linking the LGBT community to a murder that happened in Universitas Indonesia, the university I went to. The article mentioned an organization called Support Group and Resource Center on Sexuality Studies Universitas Indonesia (SGRC UI). Soon after, the university wanted the group to stop using "Universitas Indonesia" in its name because it wasn't a university-sanctioned organization. This is understandable. Then Muhammad Nasir, Minister of Research, Technology, and Higher Education, weighed in and said that gay people should not be on campuses.

"The LGBT (community) is contradictory to the Indonesian values and morals. I forbid it in all Indonesian universities under the ministry of research, technology, and higher education."

Alan Turing would be turning around in his grave.

A petition to condemn Nasir's statement was launched and he backtracked his comments in a tweet, but for better or for worse, this snowballed into a slew of hostile statements came from other public officials, including from Anies Baswedan (Minister of Education and Culture), Zulkifli Hasan

(People's Consultative Assembly speaker), and Ridwan Kamil (mayor of Bandung—the capital of West Java and Indonesia's third largest city). Kamil said he had no problems with gay people, as long as they don't publicize their movement, especially on social media. He backtracked this comment later by saying that again, he had no problems with gay people, but he had problems with pedophiles, whether straight or gay. But the damage was done. People were convinced that gays are sexual predators who will snatch away their children and turn them queer.

Fahira Idris, the Indonesian Sarah Palin, released a statement condemning the Indonesian LGBT propaganda (whatever that is). Her first sentence was that in her religion (I guess that means Islam), there is no such thing as an "LGBT concept." A few days later, Tifatul Sembiring, the former minister who said funding to help people with HIV was a waste, tweeted that according to a hadith, gay people should be killed. In Yogyakarta, after years of peaceful learning and praying, a *pesantren* (Muslim boarding house) for transwomen was shut down.

The first thing that came to my mind upon reading these statements was my friends. I asked them if they were okay (they were, so far; pissed, but okay), how many people they'd unfriended on Facebook (this varies, but a lot of them, like me, chose to do their own grassroot trolling to try to change their Facebook friends' minds). I thought of Ario. I'd lost contact with him after he'd flown away. I wondered if he was all right, if he was busy regretting his choice or if he was fighting for LGBT rights or if he was just coasting along. One of the Indonesians I approached to give his blurb on this book said that he just couldn't find the time to read the manuscript because the Indonesian queer community in such a state of emergency and he was too busy advocating and writing articles to help the cause.

But what was more painful was not the statement from Indonesia's Defense Minister, Ryamizard Ryacudu who said that LGBT cause was a modern warfare more dangerous than nuclear weapon, nor the statement from Coordinating Minister for Political, Legal and Security Affairs, Luhut Binsar Pandjaitan who said that President Joko Widodo was all ears on this issue, "but the government is in no hurry." What was more painful (and confusing) was statements from the revered Jesuit pastor, Franz Magnis Suseno and head of Indonesian Ulema Council (MUI), Din Syamsudin, who told us they were our allies, saying that queers should not be discriminated against, and then, without skipping a beat, saying that same-sex marriage should never be legalized.

Yet there are those who speak up. Forces that fight these demons. Arus Pelangi (Rainbow Current), the Indonesian gay rights group who are tirelessly fighting and advocating the queer movement in Indonesia; Irine Roba, a congresswoman from the same party that had nominated Indonesia's current president Joko Widodo, voiced out her concerns about Nasir's discriminatory remarks; and hundreds of true allies out there who're doing whatever they can. Even Ridwan Kamil did the right thing by stopping the terror group Islamic Defenders Front (FPI) from doing raids in Bandung in search of queer people. But FPI continued the raids elsewhere, and the terrorist organization, aided by the police, halted a queer empowerment seminar in Jakarta. The police shut them down, saying it was for the organizer's protection, but we knew better. If the police were really working to protect them, they would be the one guarding the door, not bashing it open.

But people are talking. We're gaining traction. There's

a blooming hope that we're witnessing the start of Indonesia's queer revolution, that this chain of events could be our Stonewall.

And here I am. Far away from the epicenter of the revolution. An armchair activist. Putting the "trolling" in "patrolling" Facebook and Twitter, writing rebuttals and linking articles on former coworkers' and classmates' homophobic remarks, telling them there's no such thing as "gay propaganda," that unlike their religion, we aren't trying to convert people. We only want to live in peace. Free to love, Free from fear.

And here I am. In a country that's also battling its own demons: presidential hopefuls who vow to take our rights, conservative lawmakers who draft misogynistic, homophobic, and transphobic bills every day. They may say that just to win votes, but there are people voting for them, meaning there are people in the third millennium, in a country as progressive as the US, who still want to treat other people not as second-class citizens, but as garbage.

And here I am. Between two realms. I'm incredibly lucky: I'm stuck in limbo, but at least I'm not in hell.